Affectionately dedicated to Martha and Tibor Rigo

Laura Ross

PUPPET SHOWS
Using Poems and Stories

Drawings by Frank Ross, Jr.

KAYE & WARD · LONDON

Other books by the author

Hand Puppets: How to Make and Use Them

Acknowledgment

We would like to thank the publishers of the following selections for their kind permission to reprint them in this collection: "The Three Billy-Goats-Gruff," from *Popular Tales From the Norse*, by Peter Christen Asbjornsen and Jorgen Moe, translated by Sir George Webbe Dasent, published by G. P. Putnam's Sons; "The Tiger, the Brâhman and the Jackal," from *The Tales of the Punjab*, by Flora Annie Steel, published by Macmillan and Co., Ltd.; "Johnny-Cake," from *English Fairy Tales*, by Joseph Jacobs, published by G. P. Putnam's Sons; and "Babushka," from *The Children Of Christmas*, by Edith Thomas, published by Bruce Humphries.

We would also like to thank Random House for permission to include "Peter and the Wolf," adapted from a Russian folktale by Sergei Prokofiev and originally published by Alfred A. Knopf.

The Macmillan Company has given us its kind permission to use "The Hare and the Tortoise," "The Fox and the Grapes," and "The Lion and the Mouse," from *The Fables of Aesop*, compiled by Joseph Jacobs and published in 1950.

"The Three Bears," from *The Arthur Rackham Fairy Book*, selected and illustrated by Arthur Rackham, is included with the kind permission of J. B. Lippincott and Company. British publisher George G. Harrap and Co., Ltd.

Grateful acknowledgment is also made to Houghton Mifflin and Company for permission to include: "The Youth and the Northwind," "The Elephant and the Blind Men," "Solomon and the Bees," by John Godfrey Saxe; "The Three Kings," by Henry Wadsworth Longfellow; "The Singing Leaves," by James Russell Lowell; and "Androcles and the Lion," translated from Apion's *The Aegyptiaca*.

First published in Great Britain by
Kaye & Ward Ltd
21 New Street, London EC2M 4NT

1972

Copyright © 1970 by Laura Ross
ISBN 0 7182 0915 X

Printed in England by Redwood Press Limited, Trowbridge, Wiltshire

Contents

Foreword   7
Introduction   9
A Note on the Poems   17
Punch and Judy   19
Little Jack Horner   21
Little Miss Muffet   22
Old King Cole   23
Mary's Lamb   24
There Was an Old Woman   26
Little Bo-peep   28
The Old Woman Who Lived in a Shoe   30
The Three Little Kittens   31
Where Are You Going, My Pretty Maid   34
The Crow and the Fox   35
The Blind Men and the Elephant   37
The Youth and the Northwind   40
Solomon and the Bees   48
The Leak in the Dike   51
Apple-Seed John   59
The Singing Leaves   65
The Little Drummer Boy   71
The Three Kings   73
Babushka   78
A Visit from St. Nicholas   82
Get Up and Bar the Door   86
The Dumb Wife Cured   90
Molly Malone   94

Sir Eglamour   96
Robin Hood and Little John   100
The Bailiff's Daughter of Islington   107
Lochinvar   111
Lady Clare   114
The Golden Glove   119
Moy Castle   123
A Note on the Stories   129
The Hare and the Tortoise   131
The Fox and the Grapes   133
The Lion and the Mouse   134
Androcles and the Lion   137
The Tiger, the Brâhman, and the Jackal   139
The Three Bears   145
Johnny-Cake   150
The Three Billy-Goats-Gruff   156
The Shepherd's Pipe   159
Peter and the Wolf   163
Christmas With the Cratchits   168
Noah's Ark   176
David and Goliath   181
The First Christmas   189
Index of Titles   191

Foreword

The purpose of this book is to provide poems and stories that permit staging of puppet shows, with little or no planning, preparation or rehearsal.

At a puppet symposium a few years ago, teachers discussed the need for more puppet plays based on special subjects like medieval times, Bible stories, or fables. Most of us do not realize that poems and stories are good sources for such performances.

The puppet stage need not present a show that has been written in the form of a play. Ballads, story poems, fables, folk tales, Bible stories, nursery rhymes, and sections of long stories may also be used.

A dramatic poem or story may be enacted with little or no word changes or omissions, and without having to be rewritten in play form or memorized. A narrator reads aloud and puppeteers manipulate the puppets to coordinate with the narration.

Folk tales and story poems, including ballads, may be dramatized in shadow plays and live pantomime, or with hand puppets because of their swift-paced dramatic qualities. They plunge into action quickly with vivid detail and, with an economy of words, everything moves swiftly toward a conclusion.

Each poem or story will be more useful to you as a puppet show if you visualize the events taking place, asking the question, "How do we show it?" The production notes following each selection will explain one way to stage it. Undoubtedly you will think of other ways that will be right for you. Only the highlights have been touched upon here to encourage you to think creatively of ways to show the plays.

Simple poems and stories for very young puppeteers have been included along with more complex selections for those with more experience. Of course, in a collection of this sort it is impossible to include all the fine works that can be used for puppet shows. One could spend a lifetime searching for such material, for the more one reads the more one finds.

With this collection as a start, perhaps the reader will explore further the many poems and stories that can be used with puppets.

Introduction

Dramatizing poems and stories is not new. Thousands of years ago, before poems and stories were written, they were recited, sung, and dramatized. It is believed that primitive man told stories with expressive gestures in the shadows of his cave. Later, ballads were sung by minstrels, who related the deeds of gallant men by singing about and dramatizing them. Thus we have inherited the oral tradition of verse and stories.

Often the full beauty of a poem or story is felt only when it is spoken aloud. The ability to pantomime and dramatize the action created by the words gives the poems and stories even more meaning. They come to life as the images are given voice, thus permitting the audience to hear, to see, to feel with the actors.

It does not matter if we do not always understand the exact meaning of a poem. Some poems have a clear meaning, some create a magic spell, some are mysterious, and some are dramatic. All are enjoyable.

Anonymous poems, like old ballads and songs, were composed by many people throughout the centuries. They were probably created long ago by individual poets, and then over a period of centuries, each generation added to or changed them.

At first, folk tales and fables were told by word of mouth. Then scholars began to record them for posterity. It seems appropriate to draw from such a literary heritage to dramatize with puppets.

The material in this collection is especially suitable for use with three basic types of performance: rod puppets used either in front of a screen or as shadow puppets behind it, papier-mâché hand puppets, and live pantomime against a large screen.

Shadow puppets are as old as the beginning of man. They may have started with the caveman putting a stick on his fire and watching the shadow the flame cast on the wall. It is easy to see how he might have used these sticks to cast shadows as a means of helping him to relate the events of his day's hunt. Perhaps he used this form of storytelling to entertain himself and his family. Here was the beginning of shadow puppets.

Shadow figures were first used on the theatrical stage in China, where they became very popular. From there they spread to Siam, Java, northern Egypt, Turkey, and Greece. They reached Western Europe in the eighteenth century.

The more popular shadow puppets are flat figures, usually shown in profile, cut out of cardboard and attached to holding rods. These figures can be held before a backdrop or screen over a table that serves as a platform. They can also be used as silhouettes if they are held behind a screen with a light shining behind them. The manipulator should be seated on the floor, keeping his head below the tabletop so that the light will not cast his shadow on the screen.

A hand puppet is a hollow figure, which is moved by thrusting one's hand into the figure and moving it with one's fingers and wrist. No doubt it also had its roots in antiquity.

Puppets were used in the Church during the Middle Ages to dramatize stories from the Bible. Then they became too theatrical, or too vulgar, and were banned by the Church. The puppet's entry into the Church and its eventual expulsion forms a major chapter in its history. Thereafter, puppeteers were to play in the streets, fair grounds, inns, and, eventually in theatres of their own.

Puppet shows in Shakespeare's England were known as "motions," and their operators as "motion men." Hand puppets travelled everywhere in medieval Europe. By the seventeenth century, motion men were travelling along with tinkers, beggers, gypsies, and ballad singers.

The most famous names in puppetry are Punch and Judy. Punch evolved over many centuries. First referred to as Pulcinello in 1600, he may have inherited his hump and hooked nose from an ancient Roman clown.

Japan's tradition of hand puppets, which is unlike any other, has its roots as far back as 1000 B.C. The Western world is most familiar with the Bunraku Japanese puppets. These are large—three-and-a-half to four-and-a-half feet tall. Three puppeteers manipulate them. The principal operator moves the head and right arm; one of his assistants moves the left arm; and the other moves the legs. Puppeteers wear black garments and hooded masks. The narrator sits below stage to the side and narrates the story. Bunraku puppeteers use highly stylized motions when manipulating their puppets and perform in perfect synchronization with the narrator.

Today, puppet performances are given in theatres as well as on television and are appreciated by people of all ages. Many innovations in the use of hand puppets have been introduced.

Pantomime is a form of drama as old as mankind and as

modern as television. A mime is an actor who develops a story by making expressive body movements and gestures, with or without the accompaniment of words or music. He conveys his thoughts and emotions to his audience through action. A pantomime is the performance itself, developed by movement and gestures.

The earliest form of pantomime, again, was probably practiced by the caveman, who, returning from the hunt, related his story to his family and friends with gestures because he could not express himself completely with the use of language. Drawings have been found on the walls of caves, showing prehistoric man performing pantomime in an attempt to influence his gods and the animals he wished to conquer. They usually showed a successful hunt, which was thought to bring good luck to the hunter.

Primitive pantomimes were performed all over the world to tell a story, to influence the gods, and sometimes to amuse. The Zuñi Indians of the American Southwest at one time danced a ceremonial dance of the corn maidens to bring rain for the corn crops. Some of the pantomime dances in the Aleutian Islands tell a mythological story or relate an event in the history of the tribe. Others are performed purely for amusement. The Hopi Indians still do a serpent dance in pantomime, telling about the struggle of the Hopi to survive when a great serpent rose from the sea and created a flood.

Pantomime eventually developed into the drama. The ancient Greeks used pantomime in their temples for ceremonial celebrations. Later they used it in the theatre. The actors wore masks and synchronized their body movements with the narration. When the influence of the Greek theatre reached Rome, both Greek myths and masks were borrowed for Roman pantomimes.

Later, the *commedia dell' arte*, established by theatre groups that had been expelled from the Church, began to perform in the streets of Italy.

The *commedia dell' arte* consisted of travelling troupes of actors who went from city to city, street to street, acting wherever they had an audience. Often they would set up their stages in the marketplaces of Italy. Pantomime was performed with mimes wearing masks and costumes of many colours. Plays were recited offstage by narrators, and the movements were performed by actors on the platforms.

Stock characters—Arlecchino, Columbina, Pantalone, Capitano, Pedrolino, and many others—performed without scripts, improvising dialogue and pantomime. Each of these stock players wore a mask representing the character he portrayed.

To the English, the *commedia dell' arte* seemed crude. English pantomime consisted of elaborate performances of folk and fairy tales in which characters in slapstick situations performed in such stories as "Harlequin and Mother Goose," "Harlequin and William Tell," "Harlequin and the Steam Engine," and many others. These plays often involved mechanical tricks and gymnastics with characters going through trap doors and windows, and taking part in other antics.

Today, we have the clown, who performs in the tradition of the slapstick pantomime. He even dresses in the original bright-coloured pattern of Harlequin.

Whether one uses rod and stick puppets, papier-mâché

puppets, or live pantomime, more than one method is possible for a performance with poems and stories:

(1) One puppeteer narrates and manipulates the puppets. This is not as easy as it sounds, since the reader's attention is divided between reading and performing. The puppeteer may be so absorbed by the words he is reciting that he forgets to move his puppets to synchronize with the narration.

(2) A reader may narrate the whole verse or story while actors interpret the action. This requires perfect synchronization between the words and action.

(3) One reader may handle the descriptive parts, while others read the dialogue of the characters. On stage, performers operate the puppets, synchronizing action with the words read. This requires more skill but is a good method to use when many characters are speaking.

(4) In a ballad (a song that tells a story), a person may sing the ballad if the music is known, while the actors manipulate the puppets. Or a chorus may sing the entire ballad pantomimed by the actors. If the music is not known, performers may give a choral reading, or a blending of many voices.

Much has been written on the techniques of pantomime. The important thing to note here is that expressive and creative action is the most important factor in this ancient, yet modern, form of drama. Human actions express feelings or show a sequence of events and emotions. Such actions can be performed either with or without words.

The language of pantomime is as creative, as inventive, as

free as that of any form of art. What is done is not as important as how it is done. To learn how to pantomime, try doing the action; observe and concentrate on what is being done. Think and concentrate on the sequence of movements in a particular action, whether it be taking off a coat or sewing a hem. Then try the action by exaggerating the movements for clarity. The style you develop in the series of motions is what makes pantomime an art.

The terms "live puppets" and "live pantomime" describe a performance acted by a living person or persons before or behind a translucent screen or white sheet. If the performance is enacted behind the screen or sheet, with a source of light placed in back of the actors, the drama becomes a shadow or silhouette play with living actors rather than stick or rod puppets.

Since a live puppet has a greater range of movement, this technique is desirable for poems and stories with a greater variety of events and movements.

Not all narrative poems, ballads, and tales are appropriate for dramatic performances. Some are more reflective than active. One must select only those that have a great deal of action and dialogue. The material must include a sequence of events that can be dramatized with imagination and creative expression. Characters found in real life are also found in poems and stories. These characters must be clearly defined: the lover, the shy maid, the bold and courageous man, the henpecked husband, the timid man, and the bully.

When reading a poem or story for use pay particular attention to the props that will be needed. This is especially true for complex stories in which props play an important role in the development. However, if a selection makes use of mechanical features, such as the smoke encircling Santa's head like a wreath in "A Visit from St. Nicholas," it is not necessary to show such mechanical happenings.

Also, wherever you feel that a slight omission of text is feasible, do not hesitate to omit it. This is known as adapting the story to suit your needs. Feel free to interpret any poem or story.

There are many different languages, interpretations, sounds, and meanings in man's world. The language of puppetry, whether it be expressed with rod puppets, hand puppets, or live pantomime, is as universal as man himself.

A Note on the Poems

This section is devoted to poems, including nursery rhymes, story poems, and ballads.

Nursery rhymes are universal. They belong to boys and girls all over the world. And what a world of characters they include: kings and queens, lords and ladies, soldiers and sailors, thieves and rogues, the miller, the baker, the candlestick maker, the peddlar, the tailor, the hunter, the old, the young, the wise, the foolish, and many animals too.

There are scholars who believe that the oldest nursery rhymes go back to ancient times, but most of those we know of today originated in the time of King Henry VIII of England.

Some of these rhymes are counting-out ditties intended to help children learn numbers and the alphabet. Some are proverbs, some nonsense rhymes, some lullabies. Some are sad, some romantic, and some are street songs.

These rhymes are known as "Nursery Rhymes" in England but as "Mother Goose" stories in France and America.

Because they make us laugh and because they are full of the drama of life, nursery rhymes—no matter how short—are a good source to draw from for the puppet stage to entertain and amuse little children.

Poetry, like art and music, is important because of what it makes us feel. Most poems depend upon visual and auditory imagery, painting pictures in our minds with words in rhythm, rhyme, or free verse.

There are many different kinds of poems: poems that tell

a story—of historical interest or of romance and adventure —called narrative or story poems; poems that are humorous nonsense; poems that present an idea or mood; poems that capture an experience; poems that are mysterious; poems that are sad or happy and gay.

The narrative, or story, poem lends itself naturally to the puppet stage because it is dramatic, moving along very quickly, and because it should be heard, and possibly seen, for better appreciation.

Ballads are narrative songs that tell a dramatic story. The best English ballads, those of the fourteenth, fifteenth, and sixteenth centuries, were sung by minstrels. There are several types of ballads: domestic tragedy, which deals with a family feud; the historical ballad, dealing with actual historical events; the outlaw ballad, which immortalizes rebels like Robin Hood of England or Jesse James of America; the ballad that laments; and the ballad that uses a love theme.

In old England there were two sources of ballads, the minstrel attached to a nobleman's court, whose ballads were written in lyrical style; and the roadside ballad, springing from the daily happenings in the lives of the common people. Ballads are romantic, thrilling, and exciting stories. They are most effective if sung or recited to the strum of a guitar. Because they are dramatic, they do very well on the puppet stage.

Punch

Punch and Judy

Punch and Judy
Fought for a pie,
Punch gave Judy
A sad blow in the eye.

Says Punch to Judy,
"Will you have more?"
Says Judy to Punch,
"My eye is sore."

PRODUCTION NOTES

Technique
Puppet stage. Papier-mâché hand puppets.

Cast
Punch—Wears patched costume, pointed cap on head with point draped down. Carries a stick.
Judy—Apron over dress. Mob cap on head.
Three narrators—Offstage. One reads descriptive lines, while the others take the parts of Punch and Judy.

Setting
Before closed curtains. Pie is made of cardboard.

Action
Footlight goes on. Punch and Judy appear from behind the curtain and start fighting for pie Judy holds. Punch whacks Judy with stick several times. Judy drops pie and places hands over her face. Footlight goes off. Punch and Judy disappear behind curtain.

Little Jack Horner

Little Jack Horner
Sat in the corner,
Eating a Christmas pie;
He put in his thumb,
And pulled out a plum,
And said, "What a good boy am I!"

PRODUCTION NOTES

Technique
Puppet stage. Jointed rod puppet silhouetted against a white screen, with a projector light behind the puppets. Shown in profile, Jack Horner is cut out of stiff cardboard.

Cast
Jack Horner—Wears a shirt and long trousers. Plum is part of his thumb. Pie is part of his lap.
One narrator—Offstage.

Setting
Silhouette of a stool made out of cardboard.

Action
Projector light goes on. Jack is seated on a stool, eating pie with his thumb. Projector light goes off.

Little Miss Muffet

Little Miss Muffet
Sat on a tuffet,
Eating her curds and whey;
There came a big spider,
Who sat down beside her
And frightened Miss Muffet away.

PRODUCTION NOTES

Technique

Puppet stage. Jointed rod puppet silhouetted against a white screen. Shown in profile, Miss Muffet is cut out of stiff cardboard.

Cast

Miss Muffet—Wears frilly pinafore. Cardboard bowl is attached to her lap.

Spider—Attached to string on rod, like mobile. Has four pairs of long legs.

One narrator—Offstage.

Setting

Silhouette of a stool made of cardboard may be seen through the screen.

Action

Projector light goes on. Miss Muffet is sitting on a stool,

eating from her bowl. Spider approaches from above. When he gets close, Miss Muffet gets up and runs away. Projector light goes off.

Old King Cole

Old King Cole
Was a merry old soul,
And a merry old soul was he;
He called for his pipe,
And he called for his bowl,
And he called for fiddlers three.

Every fiddler, he had a fiddle,
And a very fine fiddle had he;
Twee tweedle-dee, tweedle-dee, went the fiddlers,
Oh, there's none so rare,
As can compare
With King Cole and his fiddlers three!

PRODUCTION NOTES

Technique
Live pantomime behind a large white screen drawn across a stage or over an open doorway, with a projector light behind the performers. Play recording of violin music at appropriate time.

Cast
King Cole—Wears royal robes and crown.
Page—Tunic and tights.
Three fiddlers—Tunics and tights.
One narrator—Offstage.

Setting
Chair on raised platform. King uses a long-stemmed pipe.
Violins may be real or made of cardboard.

Action
Projector light goes on. King is seated on throne, his body
shaking with laughter. He gestures with his arm for his page,
who appears from side with pipe and bowl of tobacco. He
gestures for his fiddlers, who appear with their fiddles. King
fills pipe, and pretends to smoke while page holds bowl of
tobacco and fiddlers stand before him playing. King laughs
heartily. Projector light goes off.

Mary's Lamb

Mary had a little lamb,
    Its fleece was white as snow;
And everywhere that Mary went
    The lamb was sure to go.

It followed her to school one day,
    That was against the rule;
It made the children laugh and play
    To see a lamb at school.

And so the teacher turned it out,
    But still it lingered near;
And waited patiently about
    Till Mary did appear.

"Why does the lamb love Mary so?"
    The eager children cry.
"Why, Mary loves the lamb, you know,"
    The teacher did reply.

PRODUCTION NOTES

Technique

Puppet stage. Papier-mâché hand puppets. Lamb is a rod puppet cut out of cardboard with cotton pasted on it.

Cast

Mary—Wears pinafore over dress.

Girl—Dressed like Mary, with different-coloured pinafore.

Boy—Tyrolean-style braces attached to belt; Tyrolean hat with feather.

Teacher—High-necked blouse, long skirt; glasses over nose.

Lamb

Three narrators—Offstage. One reads descriptive passages, while the others read speaking parts.

Setting

School building on one side of stage. It is made of stiff cardboard and painted. Lamb is made of cardboard and covered with white absorbent cotton.

25

Action

Footlight goes on. Curtains are drawn. Teacher stands in front of school. Boy and girl enter, walking hand in hand toward school. Then they stand beside the teacher. Mary enters, with her lamb following her, and walks back and forth a few times, then toward school building. Children see lamb and laugh. Teacher waves vigorously, indicating that the lamb must leave. All disappear behind building and below stage, but lamb lingers on. Teacher, Mary, and children reappear. Curtain closes. Footlight goes off.

There Was an Old Woman

There was an old woman, as I've heard tell,
She went to the market, her eggs for to sell;
She went to market all on a market-day,
And she fell asleep on the King's highway.

There came by a pedlar whose name was Stout,
He cut her petticoats all round about;
He cut her petticoats up to the knees,
Which made the old woman shiver and freeze.

When this little old woman first did wake,
She began to shiver and she began to shake;
She began to wonder and she began to cry,
"O! deary, deary me, this is none of I!

26

"But if it be I as I hope it be,
I've a little dog at home, and he'll know me;
If it be I, he'll wag his tail
And if it be not I, he'll loudly bark and wail!"

Home went the little woman all in the dark,
Up got the little dog, and he began to bark;
He began to bark; so she began to cry,
"O! deary, deary me, this is none of I!"

PRODUCTION NOTES

Technique

Puppet stage. Papier-mâché hand puppets.

Cast

Old woman—Wears blouse, long skirt made of thin paper, and mob cap. Carries a basket with eggs.

Pedlar—Dressed in long trousers, shirt, and old hat.

Dog—Has big floppy ears.

Two narrators—Offstage. One reads the descriptive passages, while the other takes the part of the old woman.

Setting

Cardboard tree in centre of stage. Basket is made of cardboard; eggs of papier-mâché and coloured.

Action

Footlight goes on. Curtains are drawn. Old woman approaches from the left, with a basket of eggs over her arm. She stops under the tree, places the basket on ground, lies down and falls asleep. Pedlar approaches from right, looks at her and tears her paper skirt. Pedlar continues and exits at left. Old woman awakens and shivers. She looks at her torn skirt, shows surprise by throwing up her hands, then cries. She gets up and continues on her way. Dog enters from right of stage, stops before her, and barks and growls angrily. Old woman cries again, wailing and moaning. Footlight goes off. Curtain is drawn.

Little Bo-peep

Little Bo-peep has lost her sheep,
    And doesn't know where to find them;
Leave them alone, and they'll come home,
    Bringing their tails behind them.
Little Bo-peep fell fast asleep,
    And dreamt she heard them bleating;
But when she awoke, she found it a joke,
    For they were still a-fleeting.
Then up she took her little crook,
    Determined for to find them;
She found them indeed, but it made her heart bleed,
    For they'd left their tails behind them.
It happened one day, as Bo-peep did stray
    Into a meadow hard by,
There she espied their tails side by side,
    All hung on a tree to dry.
She heaved a sigh, and wiped her eye,
    And over the hillocks went rambling,

And tried what she could, as a shepherdess should,
    To tack again each to its lambkin.

PRODUCTION NOTES

Technique

Puppet stage. Bo-peep is papier-mâché hand puppet. Sheep, in profile, are cardboard rod puppets covered with cotton.

Cast

Little Bo-peep—Wears a shepherdess's dress draped and gathered at the waist, large hat. Uses a crook.

Several sheep

One narrator—Offstage.

Setting

A countryside scene appears in background. There is a tree on the left and another on the right, with bushes around it. All props are made of cardboard.

Action

Footlight goes on. Curtains are drawn. Bo-peep enters and walks back and forth, with her hand shading her eyes as she looks for her sheep. She lies down under a tree and falls asleep. We hear the sound of bleating sheep. Bo-peep gets up, picks up crook, and continues to look. Sheep appear from below stage, all with their tails missing. Bo-peep gasps in surprise. Curtain is drawn.

When curtain reopens, we see a line strung from tree to tree, with hanging tails attached with small clothes pegs. Bo-peep weeps, takes tails down, and searches for the sheep again. Curtain is closed. Footlight goes off.

The Old Woman Who Lived in a Shoe

There was an old woman who lived in a shoe;
She had so many children she didn't know what to do;
She gave them some broth without any bread;
She whipped them all soundly and put them to bed.

PRODUCTION NOTES

Technique
Puppet Stage. Papier-mâché hand puppets.

Cast
Old woman—Wears long dress, apron, and mob cap.
Several boys and girls—Girls are in different-coloured pinafores; boys wear Tyrolean-style braces attached to belt.
One narrator—Offstage.

Setting
There is a large shoe in centre of stage with trees and bushes around it. A small saucer is on the ground. A countryside can be seen in background. All props are made of cardboard.

Action
Footlight goes on. Curtains are drawn. Children are running around playing tag. Some are climbing over the shoe. Old woman frantically tries to catch them, but they dodge her. Old woman finally catches them, one by one, picks up saucer, feeds them, and whips them. Each disappears behind the shoe and below stage. Curtain is closed. Footlight goes off.

The Three Little Kittens

ELIZA LEE FOLLEN

Three little kittens lost their mittens;
  And they began to cry,
    "Oh, mother dear,
    We very much fear
That we have lost our mittens."
    "Lost your mittens!
    You naughty kittens!
Then you shall have no pie!"
        "Mee-ow, mee-ow, mee-ow."
"No, you shall have no pie."

The three little kittens found their mittens;
  And they began to cry,
    "Oh, mother dear,
    See here, see here!
See, we have found our mittens!"
    "Put on your mittens,
    You silly kittens,
And you may have some pie."
        "Purr-r, purr-r, purr-r,
Oh, let us have the pie!
        Purr-r, purr-r, purr-r."

The three little kittens put on their mittens,
  And soon ate up the pie;

"Oh, mother dear,
    We greatly fear
That we have soiled our mittens!"
    "Soiled your mittens!
    You naughty kittens!"
Then they began to sigh,
        "Mee-ow, mee-ow, mee-ow."
Then they began to sigh,
        "Mee-ow, mee-ow, mee-ow."

The three little kittens washed their mittens,
    And hung them out to dry;
        "Oh, mother dear,
        Do not you hear
That we have washed our mittens?"
    "Washed your mittens!
    Oh, you're good kittens!
But I smell a rat close by,
        Hush, hush! Mee-ow, mee-ow."
"We smell a rat close by,
        Mee-ow, mee-ow, mee-ow."

PRODUCTION NOTES

Technique
Puppet stage. Papier-mâché hand puppets.

Cast
Three kittens—Wear brown, grey, and white felt costumes.

Mother cat—Black felt costume with white apron.
Five narrators—Offstage. One reads the descriptive passages. One reads the part of the mother cat, and three, in unison, read the parts of the kittens.

Setting
Table with a pie made of thin tissue paper on it, and another table with a small wash basin and small clothes pegs on it. Under one table are three pairs of bright-red felt mittens. A thin washline is strung from one side of the puppet stage to the other. The interior of a kitchen with a stove and window with curtains can be seen in background. Tables are made of cardboard.

Action
Footlight goes on. Curtains are drawn. Kittens are crying and rubbing their eyes, while mother is scolding and shaking her finger. Kittens look around, find mittens under the table and put them on. Then each tears off a piece of pie, pretends to eat it, and quickly throws it below stage. Mother scolds kittens for soiling mittens, and they go to basin and wash their mittens. Mittens are hung on the washline with small clothes pegs. When the kittens and the mother cat smell a rat nearby they scatter, looking for it, and then they exit. The curtain is closed and the footlight goes off.

Where Are You Going, My Pretty Maid

"Where are you going, my pretty maid?"
"I'm going a-milking, sir," she said.
"May I go with you, my pretty maid?"
"You're kindly welcome, sir," she said.
"Say, will you marry me, my pretty maid?"
'Yes, if you please, kind sir," she said.
"What is your father, my pretty maid?"
"My father's a farmer, sir," she said.
"What is your fortune, my pretty maid?"
"My face is my fortune, sir," she said.
"Then I can't marry you, my pretty maid!"
"Nobody asked you, sir," she said.

PRODUCTION NOTES

Technique
Live pantomime in silhouette behind a large white screen drawn across a stage or a wide, open doorway, with a projector light behind the performers.

Cast
Pretty maid—Wears a long dress with apron and a frilly mob cap. Carries a pail.
Young man—Trousers, shirt, and hat.
Two narrators—Offstage. One for each character.

Setting
No scenery is needed.

Action

Projector light goes on. The young man enters from right; the young maid from left. They meet, and the man removes his hat and bows low. Maid coyly turns head away. He lifts her chin while talking to her. When young man refuses to marry the maid, he lifts his hands and shakes his head. Maid snaps her fingers at him, shrugs her shoulders, and walks away. Projector light goes off.

The Crow and the Fox

Aesop fable retold by JEAN DE LA FONTAINE and translated by EDWARD MARSH

A Crow sat perched upon an oak,
　　And in his beak he held a cheese.
　　A Fox snuffed up the savoury breeze,
And thus in honeyed accent spoke:

"O Prince of Crows, such grace of mien
Has never in these parts been seen.
If but your song be half as good,
You're the best singer in the wood!"

The Crow, beside himself with pleasure,
　　And eager to display his voice,
Opened his beak, and dropped his treasure.
　　The Fox was on it in a trice.

35

"Learn, sir," said he, "that flatterers live
On those who swallow what they say.
A cheese is not too much to give
For such a piece of sound advice."
The Crow, ashamed to have been such easy prey,
Swore, but too late, no one would catch him twice!

PRODUCTION NOTES

Technique

Sock puppets. Each is constructed with a large, heavy, empty
sock. The top of the toe is the head and the upper lip. The
heel of the sock is the lower lip. Decorate socks with coloured
felt for the eyes, the fox's nostrils, the crow's beak, fur, and
feathers. To manipulate puppets, insert four fingers into the
toe section, and your thumb into the heel.

Cast
Crow
Fox
One narrator—Offstage.

Setting
A green woodland with a large oak tree in the foreground.
The oak tree and the background are cut out of stiff card
board and painted.

Action
Curtain opens. A crow sits in a large oak tree with a piece of
cheese in his mouth. Below, a fox sniffs the air until he
locates the cheese. He then looks up at the crow sitting in the

tree. The fox sways his body to and fro as he makes his speech. When the crow drops the piece of cheese, the fox quickly snatches it and runs off. Curtain closes.

The Blind Men and the Elephant

JOHN GODFREY SAXE

It was six men of Indostan,
  To learning much inclined,
Who went to see the Elephant
  (Though all of them were blind),
That each by observation
  Might satisfy his mind.

The First approached the Elephant,
  And happening to fall
Against his broad and sturdy side,
  At once began to bawl:
"God bless me! but the Elephant
  Is very like a wall!"

The Second, feeling of the tusk,
  Cried, "Ho! what have we here
So very round and smooth and sharp?
  To me 'tis mighty clear
This wonder of an Elephant
  Is very like a spear!"

37

The Third approached the animal,
    And happening to take
The squirming trunk within his hands,
    Thus boldly up and spake:
"I see," quoth he, "the Elephant
    Is very like a snake!"

The Fourth reached out his eager hand,
    And felt about the knee.
"What most this wondrous beast is like
    Is mighty plain," quoth he:
" 'Tis clear enough the Elephant
    Is very like a tree!"

The Fifth, who chanced to touch the ear,
    Said: "E'en the blindest man
Can tell what this resembles most;
    Deny the fact who can,
This marvel of an Elephant
    Is very like a fan!"

The Sixth no sooner had begun
    About the beast to grope,
Than, seizing on the swinging tail
    That fell within his scope,
"I see," quoth he, "the Elephant
    Is very like a rope!"

And so these men of Indostan
   Disputed loud and long,
Each in his own opinion
   Exceeding stiff and strong,
Though each was partly in the right,
   And all were in the wrong!

So oft in theologic wars,
   The disputants, I ween,
Rail on in utter ignorance
   Of what each other mean
And prate about an Elephant
   Not one of them has seen!

PRODUCTION NOTES

Technique

Puppet stage. Papier-mâché hand puppets.

Cast

Six men of Indostan—Wear white robes and turbans.
Seven narrators—Offstage. One narrates descriptive passages, while others read the parts of the six men.

Setting

A street in India with domed Hindu palaces. Constructed of stiff cardboard and painted. A grey pâpiér-mache elephant stands in the foreground.

Action

Curtain opens.

The blind men enter in single file from the right of the puppet stage. Each has a hand on the shoulder of the one in front of him. The leader's hand is outstretched until he touches the elephant. Then each blind man takes a position around it, feeling a different part of its body. The first man feels the broad side of the elephant; the second feels the tusk; the third, the trunk; the fourth, the knee; the fifth, the ear; and the sixth, the tail. Then the men argue about their impressions of the elephant. As the narrator recites each line in the last stanza, each of the blind men speaks out, repeating his original impression of the animal. They are still arguing when the curtain falls.

The Youth and the Northwind

JOHN GODFREY SAXE

Once on a time—'twas long ago—
　　There lived a worthy dame
Who sent her son to fetch some flour,
　　For she was old and lame.

But while he loitered on the road,
　　The Northwind chanced to stray
Across the careless younker's path,
　　And stole the flour away.

"Alas! what shall we do for bread?"
  Exclaimed the weeping lad;
"The flour is gone,—the flour is gone,—
  And it was all we had!"

And so he sought the Northwind's cave,
  Beside the distant main;
"Good Mister Boreas," said the lad,
  "I want my flour again.

" 'Twas all we had to live upon,—
  My mother old and I;
Oh give us back the flour again,
  Or we shall surely die!"

"I have it not," the Northwind growled;
  "But, for your lack of bread,
I give to you this table-cloth;
  'Twill serve you well instead;

"For you have but to spread it out,
  And every costly dish
Will straight appear at your command,
  Whatever you may wish."

The lad received the magic cloth
  With wonder and delight,
And thanked the donor heartily,
  As well, indeed, he might.

Returning homeward, at an inn
    Just half his journey through,
He fain must show his table-cloth,
    And what the cloth could do.

So while he slept the knavish host
    Went slyly to his bed,
And stole the cloth,—but shrewdly placed
    Another in its stead.

Unknowing what the rogue had done,
    The lad went on his way,
And came unto his journey's end
    Just at the close of day.

He showed the dame his table-cloth,
    And told her of its power;
"Good sooth!" he cried, " 'twas well for us
    The Northwind stole the flour."

"Perhaps," exclaimed the cautious crone,
    "The story may be true;
'Tis mighty little good, I ween,
    Your table-cloth can do."

And now the younker spread it forth,
    And tried the spell. Alas!
'Twas but a common table-cloth,
    And nothing came to pass.

Then to the Northwind, far away,
    He sped with might and main;
"Your table-cloth is good for naught;
    I want my flour again!"

"I have it not," the Northwind growled,
    "But, for your lack of bread,
I give to you this little goat,
    'Twill serve you well instead;

"For you have but to tell him this.
    'Make money, Master Bill!'
And he will give you golden coins,
    As many as you will."

The lad received the magic goat
    With wonder and delight,
And thanked the donor heartily,
    As well, indeed, he might.

Returning homeward, at the inn
    Just half his journey through,
He fain must show his little goat,
    And what the goat could do.

So while he slept the knavish host
    Went slyly to the shed,
And stole the goat,—but shrewdly placed
    Another in his stead.

Unknowing what the rogue had done,
    The youth went on his way,
And reached his weary journey's end
    Just at the close of day.

He showed the dame his magic goat,
    And told her of his power;
"Good sooth!" he cried, " 'twas well for us
    The Northwind stole the flour."

"I much misdoubt," the dame replied,
    "Your wondrous tale is true;
'Tis little good, for hungry folk,
    Your silly goat can do!"

"Good Master Bill," the lad exclaimed,
    "Make money!" but, alas!
'Twas nothing but a common goat,
    And nothing came to pass.

Then to the Northwind, angrily,
    He sped with might and main;
"Your foolish goat is good for naught;
    I want my flour again!"

"I have it not," the Northwind growled,
    "Nor can I give you aught,
Except this cudgel,—which, indeed,
    A magic charm has got;

"For you have but to tell it this:
    'My cudgel, hit away!'
And, till you bid it stop again,
    The cudgel will obey."

Returning home, he stopt at night
    Where he had lodged before;
And feigning to be fast asleep,
    He soon began to snore.

And when the host would steal the staff,
    The sleeper muttered, "Stay,
I see what you would fain be at;
    Good cudgel, hit away!"

The cudgel thumped about his ears,
    Till he began to cry,
"Oh stop the staff, for mercy's sake!
    Or I shall surely die!"

But still the cudgel thumped away
    Until the rascal said,
"I'll give you back the cloth and goat,
    Oh spare my broken head!"

And so it was the lad reclaimed
    His table-cloth and goat;
And, growing rich, at length became
    A man of famous note;

He kept his mother tenderly,
    And cheered her waning life;
And married—as you may suppose—
    A princess for a wife;

And while he lived had ever near,
    To favour worthy ends,
A cudgel for his enemies,
    And money for his friends.

PRODUCTION NOTES

Technique
Puppet stage. Papier-mâché hand puppets.

Cast
Dame—Wears a long skirt and blouse.
Son—Trousers, shirt, and cap.
Northwind—Old man with long white hair and beard, in a loose, flowing white robe of thin gauze to give the impression of blowing wind when he moves.
Innkeeper—Apron.
Princess—Royal robes.

Setting
There is a cave in the back and far right. Opposite, at the far left, is the interior of an inn, with a table and chair. A shed is attached to the inn. Between the inn and the cave is a path. Props are constructed of stiff cardboard and painted. Other props are a tablecloth; food and dishes made of cardboard

and attached to rods; a cardboard goat with a string attached for pulling; two clubs, one of which is on a rod; and gold pieces on rods.

Only one scene is necessary as characters appear from and disappear below stage at appropriate times.

Action

Curtain opens. The dame limps across the stage, then disappears. The youth, in the foreground carrying a bag, walks toward the cave. The Northwind appears, snatches the bag, then disappears. The youth weeps and spreads out his arms to show that the flour is gone. When he reaches the cave, the Northwind gives him a tablecloth. The youth examines it, tucks it under his arm, and nods. On his way home, he stops at the inn and sits at the table.

The innkeeper enters and watches with amazement as the youth spreads out the tablecloth and dishes of food appear, then disappear when the food has been eaten. Later, while the youth is asleep with his head on the table, the innkeeper substitutes an ordinary tablecloth for the magic cloth and leaves.

The youth awakes and leaves the inn. His mother appears from the left, and he spreads the cloth out before her. Nothing happens. She leaves, and he kicks the cloth below stage and returns to the cave.

The entire sequence is repeated, this time with a goat that produces gold. On the youth's third trip, the Northwind gives him a club. When he returns to the inn this time, he only pretends to fall asleep. The innkeeper tries to steal the club, which is on the floor, but another appears. Manipulated from below stage, the club strikes the innkeeper repeatedly.

Finally, he disappears and returns with the stolen tablecloth and goat. The curtain closes.

The youth enters in front of the curtain, followed by his mother and his wife, who is a princess. He places one arm around each.

Solomon and the Bees

JOHN GODFREY SAXE

When Solomon was reigning in his glory,
Unto his throne the Queen of Sheba came
(So in the Talmud you may read the story).
Drawn by the magic of the monarch's fame,
To see the splendours of his court, and bring
Some fitting tribute to the mighty king.

Nor this alone; much had her Highness heard
What flowers of learning graced the royal speech;
What gems of wisdom dropped with every word;
What wholesome lessons he was wont to teach
In pleasing proverbs; and she wished, in sooth,
To know if rumour spoke the simple truth.

And straight she held before the monarch's view,
In either hand, a radiant wreath of flowers;
The one, bedecked with every charming hue,
Was newly culled from nature's choicest bowers;
The other, no less fair in every part,
Was the rare product of divinest art.

"Which is the true, and which the false?" she said.
Great Solomon was silent. All-amazed,
Each wondering courtier shook his puzzled head,
While at the garlands long the monarch gazed,
As one who sees a miracle, and fain,
For every rapture, ne'er would speak again.

While thus he pondered, presently he sees,
Hard by the casement,—so the story goes—
A little band of busy, bustling bees,
Hunting for honey in a withered rose.
The monarch smiled, and raised his royal head;
"Open the window!"—that was all he said.

The window opened at the king's command;
Within the room the eager insects flew,
And sought the flowers in Sheba's dexter hand!
And so the king and all the courtiers knew
That wreath was nature's; and the baffled queen
Returned to tell the wonders she had seen.

PRODUCTION NOTES

Technique
Puppet stage. Papier-mâché hand puppets.

Cast
King Solomon—Wears a loose robe and a crown made of
cardboard and covered with goldfoil.
Queen of Sheba—Long white flowing robe. Has shoulder-
length black hair and also wears a gold crown.

Courtiers—Loose robes.

One narrator—Offstage. Recites both descriptive passages and dialogue.

Setting

Interior of King Solomon's court. In the background there is a cut-out casement window, which reaches the floor. It is made of stiff cardboard and attached to the floor in the background. In the foreground a throne is on a raised platform under a canopy of drapes. Other props are bees made of cardboard and attached to holding rods with strings, like mobiles. Flower wreaths are made of tissue paper.

Action

Curtains open. King Solomon is seated on his throne with his courtiers around him. The Queen of Sheba enters and approaches the throne, holding two small flower wreaths before her, one over each arm. She puts her question to the king, and the courtiers shake their heads. While King Solomon is thinking, he places one finger on his chin.

Suddenly the king looks up and sees bees outside the casement window. He orders a courtier to open the window. The courtier walks to the window and pushes, pretending to open it. The bees fly directly to one of the wreaths held by queen, who acts surprised and then turns and walks off the puppet stage. Curtains close.

The Leak in the Dike

PHOEBE CARY

The good dame looked from her cottage
   At the close of the pleasant day,
And cheerily called to her little son
   Outside the door at play:
"Come, Peter! Come! I want you to go,
   While there is light to see,
To the hut of the blind old man who lives
   Across the dike, for me;
And take these cakes I made for him—
   They are hot and smoking yet;
You have time enough to go and come
   Before the sun is set."

Then the good wife turned to her labour,
   Humming a simple song,
And thought of her husband working hard
   At the sluices all day long;
And set the turf a-blazing,
   And brought the coarse black bread:
That he might find a fire at night,
   And find the table spread.

And Peter left the brother,
   With whom all day he had played,
And the sister who had watched their sports

51

In the willow's tender shade;
And told them they'd see him back before
    They saw a star in sight,
Though he wouldn't be afraid to go
    In the very darkest night!
For he was a brave, bright fellow,
    With eye and conscience clear;
He could do whatever a boy might do,
    And he had not learned to fear.
Why, he wouldn't have robbed a bird's nest
    Nor brought a stork to harm,
Though never a law in Holland
    Had stood to stay his arm!

And now with his face all glowing,
    And eyes as bright as the day
With the thoughts of his pleasant errand,
    He trudged along the way;
And soon his joyous prattle
    Made glad a lonesome place—
Alas! if only the blind old man
    Could have seen that happy face!
Yet he somehow caught the brightness
    Which his voice and presence lent
And he felt the sunshine come and go
    As Peter came and went.

And now, as the day was sinking,
    And the winds began to rise,
The mother looked from her door again,

Shading her anxious eyes,
And saw the shadows deepen
    And birds to their home come back,
But never a sign of Peter
    Along the level track.
But she said: "He will come at morning,
    So I need not fret or grieve—
Though it isn't like my boy at all
    To stay without my leave."

But where was the child delaying?
    On the homeward way was he,
And across the dike while the sun was up
    An hour above the sea.
He was stopping now to gather flowers,
    Now listening to the sound,
As the angry waters dashed themselves
    Against their narrow bound.

"Ah! well for us," said Peter,
    "That the gates are good and strong,
And my father tends them carefully,
    Or they would not hold you long!
You're a wicked sea," said Peter;
    "I know why you fret and chafe;
You would like to spoil our lands and homes;
    But our sluices keep you safe."

But hark! through the noise of waters
    Comes a low, clear, trickling sound;

And the child's face pales with terror,
  And his blossoms drop to the ground.
He is up the bank in a moment,
  And, stealing through the sand,
He sees a stream not yet so large
  As his slender, childish hand.

'Tis a leak in the dike!—He is but a boy,
  Unused to fearful scenes;
But, young as he is, he has learned to know
  The dreadful thing that means.
A leak in the dike! The stoutest heart
  Grows faint that cry to hear,
And the bravest man in all the land
  Turns white with mortal fear.
For he knows the smallest leak may grow
  To a flood in a single night;
And he knows the strength of the cruel sea
  When loosed in its angry might.

And the boy! he has seen the danger
  And, shouting a wild alarm,
He forces back the weight of the sea
  With the strength of his single arm!
He listens for the joyful sound
  Of a footstep passing nigh;
And lays his ear to the ground, to catch
  The answers to his cry.
And he hears the rough winds blowing,
  And the waters rise and fall,
But never an answer comes to him

Save the echo of his call.
He sees no hope, no succour,
    His feeble voice is lost;
Yet what shall he do but watch a wait
    Though he perish at his post!

So, faintly calling and crying
    Till the sun is under the sea;
Crying and moaning till the stars
    Come out for company;
He thinks of his brother and sister,
    Asleep in their safe warm bed;
He thinks of his father and mother,
    Of himself as dying—and dead;
And of how, when the night is over,
    They must come and find him at last;
But he never thinks he can leave the place
    Where duty holds him fast.

The good dame in the cottage
    Is up and astir with the light,
For the thought of her little Peter
    Has been with her all the night.
And now she watches the pathway,
    As yester-eve she had done;
But what does she see so strange and black
    Against the rising sun?
Her neighbours are bearing between them
    Something straight to her door;
Her child is coming home, but not
    As he ever came before!

"He is dead!" she cries, "my darling!"
   And the startled father hears,
And comes and looks the way she looks,
   And fears the thing she fears;
Till a glad shout from the bearers
   Thrills the stricken man and wife—
"Give thanks, for your son has saved our land,
   And God has saved his life!"
So, there in the morning sunshine
   They knelt about the boy;
And every head was bared and bent
   In tearful, reverent joy.

'Tis many a year since then; but still,
   When the sea roars like a flood,
The boys are taught what a boy can do
   Who is brave and true and good;
For every man in that country
   Takes his son by the hand
And tells him of little Peter,
   Whose courage saved the land.
They have many a valiant hero,
   Remembered through the years;
But never one whose name so oft
   Is named with loving tears.
And his deed shall be sung by the cradle,
   And told to the child on the knee,
So long as the dikes of Holland
   Divide the land from the sea!

Peter

PRODUCTION NOTES

Technique
Puppet stage. Papier-mâché hand puppets.

Cast
Peter—Wears Dutch cap and smock.
Peter's mother—Long skirt, blouse, apron, and Dutch cap made of white cloth. May also wear a shawl.
Peter's brother—Dressed like Peter.
Peter's sister—Dressed like Peter's mother.
Blind man—Dressed like Peter.
Peter's father—Dressed like Peter.
Two neighbours—Also dressed like Peter.
Five narrators—Offstage. One narrator reads descriptive passages, while the others read the speaking parts.

Setting
Scenery is changed by opening and closing curtains. A dike

57

is painted on cloth and attached to the curtain, which is drawn to show the outdoors. There is a high embankment with a tiny trickle of water and flowers at the base of the dike. When the curtain is opened, the interior of Peter's hut may be seen. In the far left there is a table, fireplace, chair, and an open door, all made of stiff cardboard or masonite. There is a path in front of the hut. In the background there is a dike, which is similar to the dike on the curtain.

Exits and entrances are made from the right of the stage. Sound effects, like the sound of the angry sea and trickling water leaking through the dike, may be made vocally. However, if there is a tap nearby the sound of trickling water can be made by turning it on.

Action

Curtain opens. Floodlights go on and Peter's mother calls Peter, who is playing with his brother. The two boys go into the house. The mother gives Peter cakes in a kerchief to take to the blind man, which he carries over his arm. After Peter leaves, his mother hums a tune as she busies herself with her chores at the fireplace and table.

Curtain closes. Peter walks and whistles a tune. He meets the blind man, gives him the cakes, and both exit.

The curtain opens and we see Peter's mother looking for him.

The curtain closes again, and Peter enters once more, on his journey home. Then he discovers the leak in the dike. He kneels low on the floor of the stage, to the far right, and appears to be plugging the leak with his finger. Floodlights go off and Peter exits.

The curtain opens again, showing the interior of the hut. Peter's mother is still searching for him. Two neighbours enter from the left, carrying Peter between them. All give thanks that Peter is alive, kneeling before him and shaking his hand. Curtain closes after the last stanza.

Apple-Seed John

LYDIA MARIA CHILD

Poor Johnny was bended well nigh double
With years of toil, and care, and trouble;
But his large old heart still felt the need
Of doing for others some kindly deed.

"But what can I do?" old Johnny said:
"I who work so hard for daily bread?
It takes heaps of money to do much good;
I am far too poor to do as I would."

The old man sat thinking deeply a while,
Then over his features gleamed a smile,
And he clapped his hands with a boyish glee,
And said to himself: "There's a way for me!"

He worked, and he worked with might and main,
But no one knew the plan in his brain.
He took ripe apples in pay for chores,
And carefully cut from them all the cores.

He filled a bag full, then wandered away,
And no man saw him for many a day,
With knapsack over his shoulder slung,
He marched along, and whistled or sung.

He seemed to roam with no object in view,
Like one who had nothing on earth to do;
But, journeying thus o'er the prairies wide,
He paused now and then, and his bag untied.

With pointed cane deep holes he would bore,
And in every hole he placed a core;
Then covered them well, and left them there
In keeping of sunshine, rain and air.

Sometimes for days he waded through grass,
And saw not a living creature pass,
But often, when sinking to sleep in the dark,
He heard the owls hoot and the prairie-dogs bark.

Sometimes an Indian of sturdy limb
Came striding along and walked with him;
And he who had food shared with the other,
As if he had met a hungry brother.

When the Indian saw how the bag was filled,
And looked at the holes that the white man drilled
He thought to himself 'twas a silly plan
To be planting seed for some future man.

60

Sometimes a log cabin came in view,
Where Johnny was sure to find jobs to do,
By which he gained stores of bread and meat,
And welcome rest for his weary feet.

He had full many a story to tell,
And goodly hymns that he sung right well;
He tossed up the babes, and joined the boys
In many a game full of fun and noise.

And he seemed so hearty, in work or play,
Men, women and boys all urged him to stay;
But he always said: "I have something to do
And I must go on to carry it through."

The boys who were sure to follow him round,
Soon found what it was he put in the ground;
And so, as time passed and he travelled on,
Ev'ry one called him "Old Apple-Seed John."

When'er he'd used the whole of his store,
He went into cities and worked for more;
Then he marched back to the wilds again,
And planted seed on hill-side and plain.

In cities, some said the old man was crazy;
While others said he was only lazy;
But he took no notice of gibes and jeers,
He knew he was working for future years.

61

He knew that trees would soon abound
Where once a tree could not have been found;
That a flick'ring play of light and shade
Would dance and glimmer along the glade;

That blossoming sprays would form fair bowers,
And sprinkle the grass with rosy showers;
And the little seeds his hands had spread,
Would become ripe apples when he was dead.

So he kept on travelling far and wide,
Till his old limbs failed him, and he died.
He said at the last: " 'Tis a comfort to feel
I've done good in the world, though not a great deal."

Weary travellers, journeying west,
In the shade of his trees find pleasant rest;
And they often start, with glad surprise,
At the rosy fruit that round them lies.

And if they inquire whence came such trees,
Where not a bough once swayed in the breeze,
The answer still comes, as they travel on:
"Those trees were planted by Apple-Seed John."

PRODUCTION NOTES

Technique
Live pantomime in silhouette behind a large white screen

drawn across a stage or a wide, open doorway, with a projector light behind the performers.

Cast

Apple-Seed John—Wears shirt and breeches. Carries staff and knapsack.

Woman—Pioneer-style blouse, long skirt, and bonnet.

Several boys—Shirts and breeches.

Several travellers—Shirts and long trousers.

Indian—Trousers, but no shirt; feather in hair; carries knapsack.

Two narrators—Offstage. One reads descriptive passages, while the other takes Apple-Seed John's part.

63

Setting

A log cabin on the left with garden tools leaning against it. There is a large rock nearby. On the right a cluster of buildings represents a town. Between the log cabin and town is the path over which Johnny travels. Later, this path will be lined with apple trees. All props are cut out of cardboard.

Action

Projector light goes on. Apple-Seed John is seated on the rock, thinking, his head in his hand. Then, he stands up and works with garden tools. A woman appears and pays him with apples. Johnny takes a knife out of his knapsack and cuts out the apple cores, which he places in his sack. The woman disappears and Johnny journeys on, whistling. Now and then he pauses, opens his bag, and takes out apple cores. He digs holes with his cane and plants the cores. After a while Johnny stops and lies down to sleep. Owls hoot and dogs bark.

When Johnny resumes his journey, an Indian appears and walks with him for a while. Both stop, and the Indian removes the knapsack from his shoulder and shares some bread with Johnny. The Indian looks into Johnny's bag of apple cores and watches Johnny dig holes. Then he shakes his head and leaves.

Johnny stops at a log cabin to do chores. A woman comes out and pays him with bread. Later, boys play with Johnny. When Johnny is about to leave, the woman urges him to stay, but he shakes his head and waves good-bye. The woman disappears, but the boys follow Johnny, watching him dig and plant. The boys leave and Johnny continues his journey, planting apple cores as he goes along. He reaches the city, briefly does some chores, and again continues his journey, planting the cores. To show that Johnny has died, the performer walks off the stage. The projector light goes off and apple trees are quickly brought in.

When the light is turned on again, travellers are walking back and forth, admiring the apple trees. The projector light goes off.

The Singing Leaves

JAMES RUSSELL LOWELL

I

"What fairings will ye that I bring?"
　　Said the King to his daughters three;
"For I to Vanity Fair am boun'
　　Now say what shall they be?"

Then up and spake the eldest daughter,
　　That lady tall and grand,
"Oh, bring me pearls and diamonds great,
　　And gold rings for my hand."

Thereafter spake the second daughter,
　　That was both white and red,
"For me bring silks that will stand alone,
　　And a gold comb for my head."

Then came the turn of the least daughter,
    That was whiter than thistledown,
And among the gold of her blithesome hair
    Dim shone the golden crown.

"There came a bird this morning,
    And sang 'neath my bower eaves,
Till I dreamed that his music bade me,
    'Ask thou for the Singing Leaves.' "

Then the brow of the King swelled crimson
    With a flush of angry scorn,
"Well have ye spoken, my two eldest,
    And chosen as ye were born;

"But she, like a thing of peasant race,
    That is happy binding the sheaves!"
Then he saw her dead mother in her face,
    And said, "Thou shalt have thy leaves."

II

He mounted and rode three days and nights
    Till he came to Vanity Fair;
And 'twas easy to buy the gems and the silk,
    But no Singing Leaves were there.

Then deep in the greenwood rode he,
    And asked of every tree,
"Oh, if you have ever a Singing Leaf,
    I pray you give it me!"

But the trees all kept their counsel,
    And never a word said they;
Only there sighed from the pine tops
    A music of seas far away;

Only the pattering aspen
    Made a sound of growing rain,
That fell ever faster and faster,
    Then faltered to silence again.

"Oh, where shall I find a little foot page,
    That would win both hose and shoon,
And will bring to me the Singing Leaves
    If they grow under the moon?"

Then lightly turned him Walter the page,
    By the stirrup as he ran,
"Now pledge you me the truesome word
    Of a king and gentleman,

"That you will give me the first, first thing
    You meet at your castle gate.
Then the Princess shall get the Singing Leaves,
    Or mine be a traitor's fate!"

The King's head dropt upon his breast
    A moment as it might be;
" 'Twill be my dog," he thought, and said,
    "My faith I plight to thee."

Then Walter took from next his heart
   A packet small and thin,
"Now give you this to the Princess Anne,
   The Singing Leaves are therein."

III

As the King rode in at his castle gate,
   A maiden to meet him ran—
And "Welcome, Father!" she laughed and cried
   Together, the Princess Anne.

"Lo, here the Singing Leaves," quoth he,
   "And woe, but they cost me dear!"
She took the packet, and the smile
   Deepened down beneath the tear.

It deepened down till it reached her heart,
   And then gushed up again,
And lighted her tears as the sudden sun
   Transfigures the summer rain.

And the first Leaf, when it was opened,
   Said, "I am Walter the page,
And the songs I sing 'neath thy window
   Are my only heritage."

And the second Leaf sang, "But in the land
   That is neither on earth or sea,
My lute and I are lords of more
   Than thrice this kingdom's fee."

And the third Leaf sang, "Be mine! Be mine!"
  And ever it sang, "Be mine!"
Then sweeter it sang and ever sweeter,
  And said, "I am thine, thine, thine!"

At the first Leaf she grew pale enough,
  At the second she turned aside,
At the third, 'twas as if a lily flushed
  With a rose's red heart's tide.

"Good counsel gave the bird," said she,
  "I have my hope thrice o'er.
For they sing to my very heart," she said,
  "And it sings to them evermore."

She brought to him her beauty and truth,
  And broad earldoms three,
And he made her queen of the broader lands
  He held of his lute in fee.

PRODUCTION NOTES

Technique

Puppet stage. Papier-mâché hand puppets. A sock puppet is used for the king's horse. (See page 36 for directions on making sock puppets.) The king puppet has legs so that he can straddle his horse, which he rides to the fair and then to the greenwood. The two different kinds of puppets are manipulated by the same puppeteer, who holds the king on one hand and the horse on the other.

Sock-puppet horse

Cast

King—Wears rich robes with pockets and a crown made of cardboard and covered with foil.

Horse—Sock puppet. Felt pieces can be used for eyes and ears.

King's three daughters—Rich clothing and crowns.

Walter—Tunic with pocket. King's emblem, made of foil, is attached to front.

Pedlar—Peasant clothing. Drab shirt and trousers.

Eight narrators—Offstage. One for descriptive passages, and one for each speaking part.

Setting

There are three scenes. In the first and third scenes, the action takes place before closed curtains. Curtains open for the second scene, showing the fairgrounds on the left. A pedlar stands behind his stall, on which there are trinkets: rings, silks, pearls, diamonds, and a gold comb. There are more stalls and people behind the pedlar.

On the right there is a green woodland with pine trees, ferns, and bushes. Between is a road, over which the king travels from the fair to the woodland.

The pedlar's stall is made of cardboard or masonite. The greenwood is made of stiff cardboard and painted.

Action

Standing before closed curtain, the king speaks to his three daughters. His two elder daughters are vain, while the youngest is demure. At first the king is annoyed with his youngest daughter; then he affectionately puts his arm around her.

The king leaves with his page, Walter, at his side. Curtain opens. At the fair the king purchases trinkets from the pedlar and puts them in his pocket. Afterward, he and Walter enter the wood. Walter carries the singing leaves in his pocket, wrapped in a small package, and gives them to the king after they make their agreement. Curtain closes.

Upon returning home and meeting his daughter Anne, the king is surprised. He shakes his head sorrowfully when he hands her the package of the singing leaves.

Princess Anne opens the package and removes the singing leaves one at a time. The narrators may sing the words of the leaves to the tune of a song each time. Anne is surprised, but then realizes the message of the singing leaves is the message of Walter, the page. She looks at him and drops her head shyly. In the last stanza, the princess goes to Walter and places her head on his shoulder. He puts his arms around her and both walk off the stage.

The Little Drummer Boy

ANONYMOUS

He was just a little Drummer Boy
  Come to see the new-born King
    No gifts to honour Him
    No gifts fit for a king . . .
        He asked:

71

"Shall I play for you on my drum?"
    Mary nodded . . .
        The ox and the lamb kept time.
        "I played my best for Him
        Then He smiled at me . . .
                me and my drum."

The little drummer boy

PRODUCTION NOTES

Technique

Puppet stage. Papier-mâché hand puppets. Use jointed rod puppets of stiff cardboard for the ox and lamb.

Cast

Mary—Wears long blue robe. Veil over head and shoulders.
Drummer boy—Long, ragged shepherd's smock, old cap, and long scarf. Carries small, gayly decorated cardboard drum tied around his neck and a drumstick.

72

New-born King—A small doll with outstretched hands.
Ox
Lamb
Two narrators—Offstage. One reads descriptive passages, and one reads the drummer boy's speech.

Setting
Interior of a stable with a manger. Stalls with animals' heads looking over them and rafters above the animals are painted on cardboard in the background.

Action
As the curtain opens, Mary watches the new-born King, who lies in a manger. The drummer boy enters and stands beside the manger beating his drum. The ox and lamb keep time to his drum by moving their heads and forefeet. This action continues until the end.

Someone beats a drum backstage. For variety the recording "The Drummer Boy" may be played during the action, or a few people may sing.

The Three Kings

HENRY WADSWORTH LONGFELLOW

Three kings came riding from far away,
  Melchior and Gaspar and Balthasar;
Three Wise Men out of the East were they,
And they travelled by night and they slept by day,
  For their guide was a beautiful, wonderful star.

The star was so beautiful, large and clear,
  That all the other stars of the sky
Became a white mist in the atmosphere;
And by this they knew that the coming was near
  Of the Prince foretold in the prophecy.

Three caskets they bore on their saddle-bows,
  Three caskets of gold with golden keys;
Their robes were of crimson silk, with rows
Of bells and pomegranates and furbelows,
  Their turbans like blossoming almond-trees.

And so the Three Kings rode into the West,
  Through the dusk of night, over hill and dell,
And sometimes they nodded with beard on breast,
And sometimes talked, as they paused to rest,
  With the people they met at some wayside well.

·"Of the child that is born," said Balthasar,
  "Good people, I pray you, tell us the news,
For we in the East have seen his star,
And have ridden fast, and have ridden far,
  To find and worship the King of the Jews."

And the people answered, "You ask in vain;
  We know of no king but Herod the Great!"
They thought the Wise Men were men insane,
As they spurred their horses across the plain
  Like riders in haste, and who cannot wait.

74

And when they came to Jerusalem,
   Herod the Great, who had heard this thing,
Sent for the Wise Men and questioned them;
And said, "Go down unto Bethlehem,
   And bring me tidings of this new king."

So they rode away, and the star stood still,
   The only one in the grey of morn;
Yes, it stopped,—it stood still of its own free will,
Right over Bethlehem on the hill,
   The city of David, where Christ was born.

And the Three Kings rode through the gate and the guard,
   Through the silent street, till their horses turned
And neighed as they entered the great inn-yard;
But the windows were closed, and the doors were barred,
   And only a light in the stable burned.

And cradled there in the scented hay,
   In the air made sweet by the breath of kine,
The little child in the manger lay,
The Child that would be King one day
   Of a kingdom not human, but divine.

His mother, Mary of Nazareth,
   Sat watching beside his place of rest,
Watching the even flow of his breath,
For the joy of life and the terror of death
   Were mingled together in her breast.

They laid their offerings at his feet:
  The gold was their tribute to a King;
The frankincense, with its odour sweet,
Was for the Priest, the Paraclete;
  The myrrh for the body's burying.

And the mother wondered and bowed her head,
  And sat as still as a statue of stone;
Her heart was troubled yet comforted,
Remembering what the Angel had said
  Of an endless reign and of David's throne.

Then the Kings rode out of the city gate,
  With a clatter of hoofs in proud array;
But they went not back to Herod the Great,
For they knew his malice and feared his hate,
  And returned to their homes by another way.

PRODUCTION NOTES

Technique

Live pantomime in silhouette or shadow puppets behind a large white screen drawn across a stage or a wide, open doorway, with a projector light behind performers.

Cast

Three Kings—Wear regal robes trimmed with cotton and bells. Each has a different elaborate turban.
Mary—Long gown with veil over head.
King Herod—Long robe.
Christ Child—Large doll with arms outstretched.

Several people—Biblical robes.

Several narrators—Offstage. One for Balthasar, and one for each speaking part.

Setting

There are many stars in the sky, pasted on the upper back part of the screen. All but one star are cutouts so that the projector light will shine through the openings, casting a bare outline. The one different star is a large solid silhouette and is positioned above the stable. To the left of the screen is a house and nearby a stable, also in silhouette. In the stable is a manger made of wood. The Kings' hobbyhorses are made of stiff cardboard or masonite. The boxes they carry are also made of cardboard and covered with gold foil.

Action

Projector light is turned on. The Three Kings enter from the right riding their horses. They pause briefly to speak to the people gathered. The people show they know nothing about the child by shaking their heads and spreading out their arms. The people exit on the right. The Kings travel until they find Herod, who is seated in the centre of the stage and far back. They converse, and before the Three Kings resume their journey, Herod leaves. The horses neigh as the Kings pause before the house.

The Kings see the stable, dismount, and enter. Mary is kneeling beside the Christ Child in the manger. The Kings lay their gifts before the manger slowly, one at a time. Mary bows her head each time. The Kings exit at the left side instead of going back in the direction from which they came. The recording "Silent Night, Holy Night!" may be played before the projector light is turned off.

Babushka

EDITH M. THOMAS

Babushka sits before the fire
Upon a winter's night;
The driving winds heap up the snow,
Her hut is snug and tight;
The howling winds,—they only make
Babushka's fire more bright!

She hears a knocking at the door;
So late—who can it be?
She hastes to lift the wooden latch,
No thought of fear has she;
The wind-blown candle in her hand
Shines out on strangers three.

Their beards are white with age, and snow
That in the darkness flies;
Their floating locks are long and white,
But kindly are their eyes
That sparkle underneath their brows,
Like stars in frosty skies.

"Babushka, we have come from far,
We tarry but to say,
A little Prince is born this night,
Who all the world shall sway.
Come join the search; come, go with us,
Who go our gifts to pay."

Babushka shivers at the door;
"I would I might behold
The little Prince who shall be King
But ah! the night is cold,
The wind so fierce, the snow so deep,
And I, good sirs, am old."

The strangers three, no word they speak,
But fade in snowy space!
Babushka sits before her fire,
And dreams, with wistful face:
"I would that I had questioned them,
So I the way might trace!

"When morning comes with blessed light,
I'll early be awake;
My staff in hand I'll go,—perchance,
Those strangers I'll o'ertake;
And, for the Child some little toys
I'll carry, for His sake."

The morning came, and, staff in hand,
She wandered in the snow,
She asked the way of all she met,
But none the way could show.
"It must be farther yet," she sighed;
"Then farther will I go."

And still, 'tis said, on Christmas Eve,
When high the drifts are piled,
With staff, with basket on her arm,
Babushka seeks the Child:
At every door her face is seen,—
Her wistful face and mild!

Her gifts at every door she leaves;
She bends, and murmurs low,
Above each little face half-hid
By pillows white as snow:
"And is He here?" Then, softly sighs,
"Nay, farther must I go."

PRODUCTION NOTES

Technique

Puppet stage. Papier-mâché hand puppets or shadow puppets.

Cast

Babushka—Wears long dress and kerchief on her head. Later puts on long cloak and carries staff and basket of toys.

Three Kings—Royal robes. Crowns cut out of cardboard and covered with gold foil. Long white hair and beards of cotton. Carry boxes made of cardboard and covered with silver foil.

Three narrators—Offstage. One for the descriptive passages, and one for each speaking part. All three can recite the Three Kings' lines.

Babushka

Setting

At the far left is the interior of Babushka's home. There is a fireplace and stool beside it. There is a door on one side, a window with curtains, and a table with a candle on it. At stage centre to the right of the house is the exterior of the house with high snow drifts. In the background there are a number of houses with doors and windows, painted on cardboard.

The fireplace, stool, and door are constructed of stiff cardboard. The door is attached to the side of the stage. Snow drifts are white cotton. Babushka's staff is a small twig; her light, a little candle. Sound effects are the howling winds and the knocking at the door.

All characters enter from the right of the stage.

Action

Curtain opens. Babushka, who is seated on the stool, hears knocking, walks to the door, and pushes it open. She shivers from the cold and wind while standing there. She sends the three strangers at the door away and goes back to her stool beside the fireplace and meditates. Curtains are drawn.

Curtains open. It is the following morning. Babushka still sits beside the fireplace. She then gets up and picks up her staff and a small basket of toys, which she carries over one arm. She pushes the door open and walks out into the snow. As she walks, she bends her body forward to show that she is bucking bitter winds. Babushka stops in front of the doors on the background and peers through the windows. She leaves a small toy at the doorstep of each cottage before resuming her journey. Curtain closes.

A Visit From St. Nicholas

CLEMENT C. MOORE

'Twas the night before Christmas, when all through the house
Not a creature was stirring, not even a mouse.
The stockings were hung by the chimney with care,
In hopes that St. Nicholas soon would be there.

The children were nestled all snug in their beds,
While visions of sugarplums danced in their heads;
And mamma in her kerchief, and I in my cap,
Had just settled our brains for a long winter's nap—
When out on the lawn there arose such a clatter,
I sprang from my bed to see what was the matter.

Away to the window I flew like a flash,
Tore open the shutters and threw up the sash.
The moon on the breast of the new-fallen snow
Gave the lustre of midday to objects below;
When, what to my wondering eyes should appear,
But a miniature sleigh and eight tiny reindeer,
With a little old driver, so lively and quick,
I knew in a moment it must be St. Nick!

More rapid than eagles his coursers they came,
And he whistled, and shouted, and called them by name:
"Now, Dasher! Now, Dancer! Now, Prancer and Vixen!
On, Comet! On, Cupid! On, Donder and Blitzen!
To the top of the porch, to the top of the wall,
Now, dash away, dash away, dash away all!"

As dry leaves that before the wild hurricane fly,
When they meet with an obstacle, mount to the sky,
So up to the housetop the coursers they flew,
With a sleigh full of toys—and St. Nicholas too.
And then, in a twinkling, I heard on the roof
The prancing and pawing of each little hoof.
As I drew in my head and was turning around,
Down the chimney St. Nicholas came with a bound.

He was dressed all in fur from his head to his foot,
And his clothes were all tarnished with ashes and soot;
A bundle of toys he had flung on his back,
And he looked like a peddlar just opening his pack.
His eyes, how they twinkled! His dimples, how merry!
His cheeks were like roses, his nose like a cherry;
His droll little mouth was drawn up like a bow,
And the beard on his chin was as white as the snow.

The stump of a pipe he held tight in his teeth,
And the smoke, it encircled his head like a wreath.
He had a broad face, and a little round belly
That shook, when he laughed, like a bowl-full of jelly.
He was chubby and plump—a right jolly old elf,
And I laughed when I saw him, in spite of myself;
A wink of his eye, and a twist of his head,
Soon gave me to know I had nothing to dread.

He spoke not a word, but went straight to his work,
And filled all the stockings; then turned with a jerk,
And laying his finger aside of his nose,
And giving a nod, up the chimney he rose.
He sprang to his sleigh, to his team gave a whistle,
And away they all flew like the down of a thistle.
But I heard him exclaim, ere he drove out of sight,
"Happy Christmas to all, and to all a good-night!"

PRODUCTION NOTES

Technique

Puppet stage. Papier-mâché hand puppets. Rod puppets for reindeer are attached to Santa's sleigh, which also has rod.

Cast

Two children—Wear nightgowns.

Mama—Nightgown and kerchief.

Papa—Nightgown and cap.

Santa—Bright-red suit trimmed with white cotton, beard of cotton, pipe. Carries bundle of toys.

Narrators—Offstage. One narrator or a choral group.

Setting

Interior of a house with a sloping snow-covered roof, which is also visible. There are two bedrooms divided by a partition. One room belongs to the children and has a fireplace in the background. The other is Mama and Papa's room. Above the snow-covered roof is a chimney. Children's stockings hang at the fireplace. There is a cut-out window in Mama and Papa's bedroom. Both rooms have beds made of cardboard, with pillows and covers.

Construct the house, roof, chimney, reindeer, and sleigh with cardboard or masonite. Attach cotton to the rooftop for snow. The partition separating the two bedrooms is cardboard also, as is the high window in Papa's bedroom. There is a fireplace in the children's bedroom, also made of cardboard; and the chimney above it and the roof are visible to the audience.

Action

The curtain opens. The narrator or choral group begins the poem. In one bedroom Mama and Papa are sleeping; in the other, the two children. All are covered with blankets. Sleigh bells jingle as the reindeer appear in the sky pulling Santa's sleigh. When Papa hears them, he jumps out of bed, goes to the window and pretends to throw up the sash. He looks out and up and sees the reindeer and Santa. When the reindeer land on the roof, they can be heard pawing.

Santa leaves his sleigh on the roof, as he gets out of the sleigh and goes behind and down the chimney. The Santa puppet is quickly swung behind the back of the stage and around to appear in front of the fireplace. The reindeer wait on the roof. The narrator, or chorus, pauses briefly while Santa takes toys out of his bag and fills the stockings. Santa puppet is swung around and behind the fireplace to indicate that he is going up the chimney. He appears on top of the roof, climbs into his sleigh, and drives away. The chorus, if one is used, sends him off with a loud farewell. Curtain closes.

Get Up and
Bar the Door

ANONYMOUS

It fell about the Martinmas time,
   And a gay time it was then,
When our goodwife got puddings to make,
   And she's boiled them in the pan.

86

The wind so cold blew south and north,
   And blew into the floor;
Quoth our goodman to our goodwife,
   "Get up and bar the door."

"My hand is in my household work,
   Goodman, as ye may see;
And it will not be barred for a hundred years,
   If it's to be barred by me!"

They made a pact between them both,
   They made it firm and sure,
That whosoe'er should speak the first,
   Should rise and bar the door.

Then by there came two gentlemen,
   At twelve o'clock at night,
And they could see neither house nor hall,
   Nor coal nor candlelight.

"Now whether is this a rich man's house,
   Or whether is it a poor?"
But never a word would one of them speak,
   For barring of the door.

The guests they ate the white puddings,
   And then they ate the black;
Tho' much the goodwife thought to herself,
   Yet never a word she spake.

Then said one stranger to the other,
  "Here, man, take ye my knife;
Do ye take off the old man's beard,
  And I'll kiss the goodwife."

"There's no hot water to scrape it off,
  And what shall we do then?"
"Then why not use the pudding broth,
  That boils into the pan?"

O up then started our goodman,
  An angry man was he;
"Will ye kiss my wife before my eyes!
  And with pudding broth scald me!"

Then up and started our goodwife,
  Gave three skips on the floor:
"Goodman, you've spoken the very first word!
  Get up and bar the door!"

PRODUCTION NOTES

Technique

Live pantomime in silhouette against a white screen drawn across a stage or a wide, open doorway, with projector light behind the performers. Incidental music may be introduced by playing a record of Scottish bagpipes at the end when the goodwife skips around.

Cast

Man—Wears tam o' shanter, muffler, jacket, and trousers. Has beard and sideburns of felt.

Wife—Full skirt, blouse, and big apron.

Two strangers—Cloaks, boots, and large hats. One has knife made of cardboard in belt.

Five narrators—Offstage. One for descriptive passages and one for each speaking part. Use Scottish accents.

Setting

Table and two chairs in silhouette. On the table is a large wooden bowl, spoons, and a pan. There is a door to the side, which is wide open. The door is constructed of cardboard and attached at the side with slackened broad masking tape.

Action

Projector light goes on. The man and wife are seated at the table, facing each other. She is stirring the contents of the bowl and pouring it into the saucepan. He rubs his hands and knuckles and stamps his feet because he is cold. This continues until the man tells his wife to get up and bar the door, pointing to it with his thumb. The wife stops only long enough to wag her finger at him and shake her head. They pound the table with their fists while making their pact.

Strangers enter and walk to the table. Man and wife show surprise but are determined not to talk. The first stranger walks around, investigating the room while the second stranger looks at the contents in the bowl. They eat the pudding. The goodman and goodwife draw closer together as though they are afraid of the strangers, but they do not speak.

When one of the strangers takes his knife and attempts to cut off the man's beard, goodman pushes the stranger away and speaks. The wife is so happy that her husband has spoken first that she skips around, instructing her husband to shut the door. Projector light goes off.

The Dumb Wife Cured

ANONYMOUS

There was a bonny blade
Had wed a country maid,
And safely conducted her
Home, home, home.
She was neat in every part,
And she pleased him from the start,
But, ah and alas, she was
Dumb, dumb, dumb.

She was bright as the day,
And as brisk as the May,
And as round and as plump as a
Plum, plum, plum;
But still the silly swain
Could do nothing but complain
Because that his wife was
Dumb, dumb, dumb.

She could brew, she could bake,
She could sew, and she could make,
She could sweep the house with a
Broom, broom, broom;
She could wash and she could wring,
Could do any kind of thing,
But, ah, alas, she was
Dumb, dumb, dumb.

To the doctor then he went
For to give himself content,
And to cure his wife of the
Mum, mum, mum:
"Oh, it is the easiest part
That belongs unto my art,
For to make a woman speak that is
Dumb, dumb, dumb."

To the doctor he did her bring
And he cut her cattering string,
And at liberty he set her
Tongue, tongue, tongue;
Her tongue began to walk,
And she began to talk
As though she had never been
Dumb, dumb, dumb.

Her faculty she found
And she filled the house with sound,
And she rattled in his ears like a
Drum, drum, drum:
She bred a deal of strife,
Made him weary of his life,
He'd give anything again she was
Dumb, dumb, dumb.

To the doctor then he goes
And thus he vents his woes,
"Oh, doctor, you've me un-
Done, done, done,
For my wife she's turned a scold,
And her tongue can never hold,
I'd give any kind of thing she was
Dumb, dumb, dumb."

"When I did undertake
To make thy wife to speak,
It was a thing eas-i-ly
Done, done, done,
But 'tis past the art of man,
Let him do whate'er he can
For to make a scolding woman hold her
Tongue, tongue, tongue."

PRODUCTION NOTES

Technique
Live pantomime against a white screen drawn across a stage

92

or a wide, open doorway, with a projector light behind the performers.

Cast

Dumb wife—Wears a long dress, padded for plumpness, and headpiece.

Husband—Tights and short tunic.

Doctor—Long robe.

Narrators—Offstage. Choral group for descriptive passages, one for the husband, and one for doctor.

Setting

On the left there are a table and two chairs. A wooden bowl and spoons are on the table. A tablecloth that needs mending is draped over arm of a chair. A broom stands in the corner of the room. There is a cut-out window with curtains in the background. On the right is the interior of the doctor's office. It contains a table with several bottles and tongue depressors on it. There are two chairs, one for the patient and one for the doctor.

Action

Projector light goes on. While the wife and husband begin to pantomime, the doctor enters his office on the right, sits at the table, and begins to read a book. When the chorus reads that the wife is "bright as the day and brisk as the May," the wife dances around with her husband. Later, she bakes, sews, sweeps, and stirs the batter in the wooden bowl. The husband takes his wife to the doctor, and she sits in the chair while he looks into her mouth with a tongue depressor and then pretends to operate.

After she has been cured, she chatters endlessly both at the doctor's office and at home while the husband covers his ears. This action could be long and drawn out, while the narrators pause.

The husband returns to the doctor's office. The wife continues to chatter while the doctor shakes his head, shrugs his shoulders, and throws up his hands. Then he covers his ears. Projector light goes off.

Molly Malone

ANONYMOUS

In Dublin's fair city where the girls are so pretty
There once lived a maiden named Molly Malone,
And she wheeled a wheelbarrow through streets wide and
 narrow,
Cryin', "Cockles and mussels, alive, alive, oh!"

She was a fishmonger, and faith! 'twas no wonder,
For her father and mother were fishmongers, too.
And they wheeled a wheelbarrow through streets wide and
 narrow,
Cryin', "Cockles and mussels, alive, alive, oh!"

And she died of a fever of which none could relieve her,
And that was the end of sweet Molly Malone.
Now her ghost wheels her barrow through streets wide and
 narrow,
Cryin', "Cockles and mussels, alive, alive, oh!
Alive, alive, oh! Alive, alive, oh!"
Cryin', "Cockles and mussels, alive, alive, oh!"

Molly Malone

PRODUCTION NOTES

Technique

Live pantomime in silhouette behind a large white screen
drawn across a stage or a wide, open doorway, with a projector light behind performers. Someone may read or sing
the ballad to the popular folk tune accompanied by guitar,
or play the recording entitled "The Best of Burl Ives." The
audience could join in the singing of the refrain.

Cast

Molly Malone—Wears skirt, short apron, blouse, and cap
or kerchief. Barefoot.

One narrator—Offstage.

95

Setting

Silhouetted in the background are cut-out houses, with narrow and wide streets between the rows of houses. Wheelbarrow is made of cardboard or masonite.

Action

Projector light goes on. Molly Malone is pushing a wheelbarrow back and forth with one hand cupped over her mouth singing the refrain. When she dies of a fever, the projector light simply goes off for a few seconds and then turns on again, when we imagine we see Molly's ghost. Projector light goes off.

Sir Eglamour

ANONYMOUS

Sir Eglamour, that worthy knight,
He took his sword and went to fight;
And as he rode both hill and dale,
Armed upon his shirt of mail,
A dragon came out of his den,
Had slain, God knows how many men!

When he espied Sir Eglamour,
Oh, if you had but heard him roar,
And seen how all the trees did shake,
The knights did tremble, horse did quake,
The birds betake them all to peeping—
It would have made you fall a-weeping!

96

But now it is in vain to fear,
Being come unto, "Fight dog! Fight bear!"
To it they go and fiercely fight
A live-long day from morn till night.
The dragon had a plaguy hide,
And could the sharpest steel abide.

No sword will enter him with cuts,
Which vexed the knight unto the guts;
But, as in choler he did burn,
He watched the dragon a good turn;
And, as a-yawning he did fall,
He thrust his sword in, hilts and all.

There, like a coward, he to fly
Unto his den that was hard by;
And there he lay all night and roared.
The knight was sorry for his sword,
But, riding thence, said, "I forsake it,
He that will fetch it, let him take it!"

PRODUCTION NOTES

Technique

Puppet stage. Papier-mâché hand puppet for the knight,
with or without legs. The knight straddles a horse, which is
either a sock puppet (For directions on making sock puppets, see page 36.) or a hobbyhorse constructed of stiff
cardboard. If a sock puppet is used, the horse is moved with
one hand. The other hand, holding the knight, straddles it.

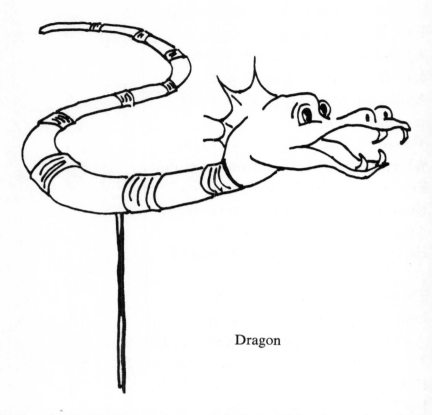

Dragon

If a small hobbyhorse is used, it is held in the palm of the same hand that holds and moves the knight.

A dragon puppet is made with segments of bamboo, each attached to the other with a piece of slackened adhesive or masking tape. Pierce a hole (for the sword) in the tape between the first and second segments. Construct the head with papier-mâché and attach with tape. Attach a holding rod at the centre section so that the dragon will wriggle and writhe when slowly shaken.

This selection could also be dramatized in pantomime in front of a large screen.

Cast

Sir Eglamour—Wears aluminium-foil shirt that looks like mail. Carries a shield and sword of cardboard covered with aluminium foil.

Horse—If a sock puppet, decorate with foil trappings. Use felt for eyes, ears and mouth.

Dragon

One narrator—Offstage.

Setting

We see a wooded area with trees and birds perched on them. On the right there is a cave with a wide opening and bushes around it. A woodland scene is painted in the background.

Construct trees and birds with stiff cardboard. The cave can be made with papier-mâché.

Action

Curtain opens. Sir Eglamour enters from the left. He rides about and then sees a dragon emerging from below stage in front of the cave. The dragon roars, frightening the knight and horse. Both tremble. Sir Eglamour becomes courageous, and prepares to do battle with the dragon. He waves his sword several times, then succeeds in thrusting it into the opening between the first two segments, where it remains. The dragon roars and disappears below stage. The knight rides off without his sword, while the dragon roars. Curtain closes.

99

Robin Hood and Little John

ANONYMOUS

When Robin Hood was about twenty years old,
   He happened to meet Little John,
A jolly, brisk blade, right fit for the trade,
   For he was a lusty young man.

Though he was called Little, his limbs they were large,
   And his stature was seven foot high;
Wherever he came, they quaked at his name,
   For soon he would make them fly.

How they came acquainted, I'll tell you in brief,
   If you would but listen awhile;
For this very jest, among all the rest,
   I think it may cause you to smile.

They happened to meet on a long, narrow bridge,
   And neither of them would give away;
Quoth bold Robin Hood, and sturdily stood,
   "I'll show you right Nottingham play!"

"Thou talkest like a coward," the stranger replied;
   "Well armed with a long bow you stand,
To shoot at my breast, while I, I protest,
   Have naught but a staff in my hand."

"The name of a coward," quoth Robin, "I scorn!
    Wherefore my long bow I'll lay by;
And now, for thy sake, a staff will I take,
    The truth of thy manhood to try."

Then Robin stept to a thicket of trees,
    And chose him a staff of ground oak;
Now this being done, away he did run
    To the stranger, and merrily spoke.

"Lo, see my staff is lusty and tough!
    Now here on the bridge we will play;
Whoever falls in, the other shall win
    The battle, and so we'll away."

"With all my whole heart," the stranger replied;
    "I scorn in the least to give out."
This said, they fell to't without more dispute,
    And their staffs they did flourish about.

At first Robin he gave the stranger a bang,
    So hard that he made his bones ring;
The stranger he said, "This must be repaid,
    I'll give you as good as you bring;

"So long as I am able to handle a staff,
    To die in your debt, friend, I scorn."
Then to it each goes, and followed their blows,
    As if they had been threshing of corn.

101

The stranger gave Robin a crack on the crown,
   Which caused the blood to appear;
Then Robin, enraged, more fiercely engaged,
   And followed his blows more severe.

So thick and so fast did he lay it on him,
   With a passionate fury and ire,
At every stroke he made him to smoke,
   As if he had been all on fire.

Oh, then into fury the stranger he grew,
   And gave him a furious look,
And with it a blow, that laid him full low,
   And tumbled him into the brook!

"I prithee, good fellow, where art thou now?"
   The stranger, in laughter, he cried.
Quoth bold Robin Hood, "Good faith, in the flood,
   And floating along with the tide!

"I needs must acknowledge thou art a brave soul,
   With thee I'll no longer contend;
For needs must I say, thou hast got the day;
   Our battle shall be at an end."

Then unto the bank he did presently wade,
   And pulled himself out by a thorn;
Which done, at the last he blew a loud blast
   Straightway on his fine bugle horn.

The echo of which through the valleys did fly,
   At which his stout bowmen appeared,
All clothed in green, most gay to be seen,
   So up to their master they steered.

"Oh, what is the matter?" quoth William Stutly.
   "Good master, you are wet to the skin."
"No matter," quoth he, "the lad which you see
   In fighting hath tumbled me in."

"He shall not go scot-free," the others replied.
   So straightway they were seizing him there,
To duck him likewise; but Robin Hood cries,
   "He is a stout fellow, forbear.

"There's no one shall wrong thee, friend, be not afraid;
   These bowmen upon me do wait;
There's three score and nine; if thou wilt be mine,
   Thou shalt have my livery straight,

"And other accoutrements fit for a man;
   Speak up, jolly blade, never fear;
I'll teach you also the use of the bow,
   To shoot at the fat fallow deer."

"Oh, here is my hand," the stranger replied,
   "I'll serve you with all my whole heart;
My name is John Little, a man of good mettle;
   Ne'er doubt me, for I'll play my part."

103

"His name shall be altered," quoth William Stutly,
    "And I will his godfather be;
Prepare, then, a feast, and none of the least,
    For we will be merry," quoth he.

He was, I must tell you, but seven foot high
    And maybe an ell in the waist—
A sweet pretty lad; much feasting they had;
    Bold Robin the christening graced,

With all his bowmen, which stood in a ring,
    And were of the Nottingham breed;
Brave Stutly came then, with seven yeomen,
    And did in this manner proceed:

"This infant was called John Little," quoth he;
    "Which name shall be changed anon;
The words we'll transpose, so wherever he goes,
    His name shall be called Little John."

Then Robin took the pretty sweet babe,
    And clothed him from top to toe,
In garments of green, most gay to be seen,
    And gave him a curious long bow.

"Thou shalt be an archer, as well as the best,
    And range in the greenwood with us;
Where we'll not want gold nor silver, behold,
    While others have aught in their purse."

Then music and dancing did finish the day;
　At length, when the sun waxed low,
Then all the whole train the grove did refrain,
　And unto their caves they did go.

And so, ever after, as long as he lived,
　Although he was proper and tall,
Yet, nevertheless, the truth to express,
　Still Little John they did him call.

PRODUCTION NOTES

Technique

Puppet stage. Papier-mâché hand puppets. Little John is
large. This ballad may also be presented in live pantomime
silhouetted against a white screen drawn across a stage or a
wide, open doorway, with a projector light behind the performers.

Someone could sing the ballad, set to music by Grace
Castagnetta, before the show.

Cast

Robin Hood—Wears green tights (for pantomime), short
green tunic with thong around waist, and green hat with
feather. Carries bow and arrows over one shoulder, a horn
over the other. All are made of cardboard.

Little John—Brown tunic and tights (for pantomime). Carries a long staff. Later wears a green cloak.

William Stutly—Short green tunic with thong at waist and
green tights (for pantomime).

Several of Robin Hood's men—Dressed like William Stutly.
Four narrators—Offstage. One reads descriptive passages,
and one reads each of the speaking parts. A narrator may
strum the guitar during the descriptive passages.

Setting
A woodland with a long, narrow log spanning a brook in the
centre. Props and background are constructed of cardboard
and painted. The brook is crushed aluminium foil, and the
log bridge can be a stick. A stick lies beside the brook for
Robin Hood to use as a staff. A doe, carried by Robin

106

Hood's men later, is made of papier-mâché and suspended from a stick.

Action
The first stanza and part of the second are performed before drawn curtains. The curtain opens in the middle of the second stanza.

Robin Hood and Little John meet and challenge each other, then attempt to push each other off the log bridge. Standing on the log, they battle vigorously with their staffs. At first one appears to be victorious, then the other, until Little John knocks Robin Hood into the brook. Both Little John and Robin Hood laugh. Robin blows his horn and summons his merry men. They seize Little John and begin to duck him in the brook, but Robin Hood quickly stops them. Little John joins the band of merry men. The narrator pauses and they all march off, returning with a doe suspended from a pole over the shoulders of two men. At the end, a guitar may be strummed while all characters dance around merrily. Curtain closes.

The Bailiff's Daughter of Islington

ANONYMOUS

There was a youth, and a well-loved youth,
    And he was a squire's son;
He loved the bailiff's daughter dear,
    That lived in Islington.

Yet she was coy and would not believe
   That he did love her so,
And not at any time would she
   A favour to him show.

But when his friends did understand
   His fond and foolish mind,
They sent him up to London
An apprentice for to bind.

And when he had been seven long years,
   And never his love could see—
"Many a tear have I shed for her sake,
   When she little thought of me."

Then all the maids of Islington
   Went forth to sport and play,
All but the bailiff's daughter dear;
   She secretly stole away.

She pulled off her gown of green,
   And put on ragged attire,
And to fair London she would go
   Her true love to inquire.

And as she went along the high road,
   The weather being hot and dry,
She sat her down upon a green bank,
   And her true love came riding by.

She started up, with colour so red,
    Catching hold of his bridle rein;
"One penny, one penny, kind sir," she said,
    "Will ease me of much pain."

"Before I give you one penny, sweetheart,
    Pray tell me where you were born,"
"At Islington, kind sir," said she,
    "Where I have had many a scorn."

"I pray thee, sweetheart, then tell to me
    O tell me, whether you know
The bailiff's daughter of Islington."
    "She is dead, sir, long ago."

"If she be dead, then take my horse,
    My saddle and bridle also;
For I will into some far country,
    Where no man shall me know."

"O stay, O stay, thou goodly youth,
    She standeth by thy side;
She is here alive, she is not dead,
    And ready to be thy bride."

"O farewell grief, and welcome joy,
    Ten thousand times therefore;
For now I have found my own true love,
    Whom I thought I should never see more."

PRODUCTION NOTES

Technique

Live pantomime against a white screen across a stage or a wide, open doorway, with projector light behind performers.

Cast

Bailiff's daughter—Wears long gown and high, pointed hat of cardboard, with veil attached at top.

Squire's son—Tights and short tunic.

Three young men—Dressed like squire's son.

Three maids—Dressed like bailiff's daughter.

Three narrators—Offstage. One for descriptive passages, and one for each speaking part.

Setting

No scenery is necessary. However, the youth rides a large hobbyhorse constructed of stiff cardboard or masonite.

Action

Projector light goes on. Youth is on bended knee with hands over his heart. He extends them toward bailiff's daughter, who shyly turns away. This is repeated several times. Youth's friends enter from right, help him to his feet, and leave with him. Bailiff's daughter exits at left. Projector light is turned off briefly to show passing of seven years.

Light goes on. Youth is crying with his arm covering his eyes. He exits at right. Bailiff's daughter enters from left, dressed in a ragged shawl. She walks back and forth for a while, then sits on the floor. Youth enters from the right on a hobbyhorse. Maid jumps up, catching the horse's reins. They talk and gesture with their arms. Youth finally dismounts and embraces maid. Projector light goes off.

110

Lochinvar

SIR WALTER SCOTT

O, young Lochinvar is come out of the west,
Through all the wide Border his steed was the best;
And save his good broadsword he weapons had none,
He rode all unarm'd and he rode all alone.
    So faithful in love and so dauntless in war,
    There never was knight like the young Lochinvar.

He staid not for brake, and he stopp'd not for stone,
He swam the Eske river where ford there was none;
But ere he alighted at Netherby gate,
The bride had consented; the gallant came late:
    For a laggard in love and a dastard in war,
    Was to wed the fair Ellen of brave Lochinvar.

So boldly he enter'd the Netherby Hall,
Among bride's-men and kinsmen and brothers and all:
Then spoke the bride's father, his hand on his sword,
(For the poor craven bridegroom said never a word):
    "O come ye in peace here, or come ye in war,
    Or to dance at our bridal, young Lord Lochinvar?"

"I long woo'd your daughter, my suit you denied;
Love swells like the Solway, but ebbs like its tide—
And now am I come, with this lost love of mine,
To lead but one measure, drink one cup of wine.
    There are maidens in Scotland more lovely by far,
    That would gladly be bride to the young Lochinvar."

The bride kiss'd the goblet: the knight took it up,
He quaff'd off the wine, and he threw down the cup.
She look'd down to blush and she look'd up to sigh,
With a smile on her lips, and a tear in her eye.
    He took her soft hand ere her mother could bar,
    "Now tread we a measure!" said young Lochinvar.

So stately his form, and so lovely her face,
That never a hall such a galliard did grace;
While her mother did fret, and her father did fume,
And the bridegroom stood dangling his bonnet and plume;
    And the bride-maidens whispered, " 'Twere better by far,
    To have matched our fair cousin with young Lochinvar."

One touch to her hand, and one word in her ear,
When they reach'd the hall-door, and the charger stood
    near;
So light to the croup the fair lady he swung,
So light to the saddle before her he sprung!
    "She is won! We are gone, over bank, bush and scaur;
    They'll have fleet steeds that follow!" quoth young Loch-
    invar.

There was mounting 'mong Graemes of the Netherby clan;
Forsters, Fenwicks and Musgraves, they rode and they ran:
There was racing and chasing, on Cannobie Lee,
But the lost bride of Netherby ne'er did they see.
    So daring in love, and dauntless in war,
    Have ye e'er heard of gallant like young Lochinvar?

PRODUCTION NOTES

Technique

Live pantomime in silhouette against a large white screen drawn across a stage or wide, open doorway, with a projector light behind performers.

Cast

Lochinvar—Wears knight's clothing with cardboard sword at his side.

Bride—Long, flowing gown and high pointed hat of cardboard with long thin veil attached at top.

Bridegroom—Tights, short tunic, and plumed hat.

Bride's father—Tights and short tunic. Carries cardboard sword at his side.

Bride's mother—Long gown, high pointed hat.

Bride's brothers—Tights and short tunics.

Several bridal guests—Men: tights and short tunics; women: long gowns, high pointed hats.

Five narrators—Offstage. One for descriptive passages, and one for each speaking part.

Setting

In the far-left corner, the interior of a lord's castle is silhouetted. Beyond a cardboard partition stand group of hobbyhorses outside hall. Inside there is a small table, with a goblet on it. The hobbyhorses are made of stiff cardboard or masonite.

Action

Projector light goes on. The bride and bridegroom are surrounded by the bride's father, mother, brothers, and guests.

113

On the far right, Lochinvar enters, riding his horse. Lochin var dismounts and enters the hall. He speaks to the group then drinks from the goblet. Later he dances with the bride During the dance, a musical record may be played. A minuet would be appropriate. Bridesmaids, standing on one side whisper behind their hands and nod. When the music stops the narration resumes. Then Lochinvar and the maid reach the hall door, run out, mount the horse, and ride away There is excitement and commotion among the guests. The men run out to chase the couple. Projector light goes off The record is played once more.

Lady Clare

ALFRED, LORD TENNYSON

It was the time when lilies blow
   And clouds are highest up in air;
Lord Ronald brought a lily-white doe
   To give his cousin, Lady Clare.

I trow they did not part in scorn:
   Lovers long-betroth'd were they:
They too will wed the morrow morn:
   God's blessing on the day!

"He does not love me for my birth,
   Nor for my lands so broad and fair;
He loves me for my own true worth,
   And that is well," said Lady Clare.

In there came old Alice the nurse;
　　Said: "Who was this that went from thee?"
"It was my cousin," said Lady Clare;
　　"To-morrow he weds with me."

"O God be thank'd!" said Alice the nurse,
　　"That all comes round so just and fair:
Lord Ronald is heir of all your lands,
　　And you are not the Lady Clare."

"Are ye out of your mind, my nurse, my nurse,"
　　Said Lady Clare, "that ye speak so wild?"
"As God's above," said Alice the nurse,
　　"I speak the truth: you are my child.

"The old Earl's daughter died at my breast;
　　I speak the truth, as I live by bread!
I buried her like my own sweet child,
　　And put my child in her stead."

"Falsely, falsely have ye done,
　　O mother," she said, "if this be true,
To keep the best man under the sun
　　So many years from his due."

"Nay now, my child," said Alice the nurse,
　　"But keep the secret for your life,
And all you have will be Lord Ronald's
　　When you are man and wife."

"If I'm a beggar born," she said,
    "I will speak out, for I dare not lie.
Pull off, pull off the brooch of gold,
    And fling the diamond necklace by."

"Nay now, my child," said Alice the nurse,
    "But keep the secret all ye can."
She said: "Not so: but I will know
    If there be any faith in man."

"Nay now, what faith?" said Alice the nurse,
    "The man will cleave unto his right."
"And he shall have it," the lady replied,
    "Though I should die to-night."

"Yet give one kiss to your mother dear!
    Alas, my child, I sinn'd for thee."
"O mother, mother, mother," she said,
    "So strange it seems to me.

"Yet here's a kiss for my mother dear,
    My mother dear, if this be so,
And lay your hand upon my head,
    And bless me, mother, ere I go."

She clad herself in a russet gown,
    She was no longer Lady Clare:
She went by dale, she went by down,
    With a single rose in her hair.

The lily-white doe Lord Ronald had brought
  Leapt up from where she lay,
Dropt her head in the maiden's hand,
  And follow'd her all the way.

Down stept Lord Ronald from his tower:
  "O Lady Clare, you shame your worth!
Why come you drest like a village maid,
  That are the flower of the earth?"

"If I come drest like a village maid,
  I am but as my fortunes are:
I am a beggar born," she said,
  "And not the Lady Clare."

"Play me no tricks," said Lord Ronald,
  "For I am yours in word and deed.
Play me no tricks," said Lord Ronald,
  "Your riddle is hard to read."

O and proudly stood she up!
  Her heart within her did not fail:
She look'd into Lord Ronald's eyes,
  And told him all her nurse's tale.

He laugh'd a laugh of merry scorn:
  He turn'd and kissed her where she stood:
"If you are not the heiress born,
  And I," said he, "the next in blood—

"If you are not the heiress born,
    And I," said he, "the lawful heir,
We two will wed to-morrow morn,
    And you shall still be Lady Clare."

PRODUCTION NOTES

Technique

Live pantomime in silhouette against a large white screen drawn across a stage or a wide, open doorway, with a projector light behind the performers. A guitar may be strummed to set the mood.

Cast

Lady Clare—Wears a rich gown, brooch, and necklace. Later, as a village maid, she wears a long shawl.
Lord Ronald—Richly clad in pants and jacket, with lace at neck and cuffs, a large plumed hat.
Nurse—Long dress and large apron and mob cap.
Four narrators—Offstage. One for descriptive passages, and one for each speaking part.

Setting

Interior of lord's castle on one side is a cut-out cardboard casement window with three branches showing through it. In the opposite corner is Lord Ronald's tower, also made of cardboard. The life-sized doe, a symbol of love, is made of stiff cardboard or masonite and drawn by a string.

Action

The projector light goes on. In one corner Lord Ronald presents Lady Clare with a doe. This should be acted with a

118

great deal of freedom, with each movement emphasized for effect. Lord Ronald leaves, and Alice the nurse enters. After Alice tells the truth about Lady Clare's birth, Lady Clare flings off her brooch and necklace with scorn. She asks for her mother's blessing, kneeling at her feet. Alice leaves, and Lady Clare walks to Lord Ronald's tower. After she meets him and reveals her true identity, Lord Ronald embraces Lady Clare, who puts her head on his shoulder. Projector light goes off.

The Golden Glove

ANONYMOUS

A wealthy young squire of Tamworth we hear,
He courted a nobleman's daughter so fair;
To marry this lady it was his intent,
All friends and relations gave gladly consent.

The time was appointed for their wedding day,
A young farmer chosen to give her away;
As soon as the farmer this lady did spy,
He inflamed her heart; "Oh my heart!" she did cry.

She turned from the squire, but nothing she said;
Instead of being married she took to her bed.
The thought of the farmer ran sore in her mind;
A way to secure him she quickly did find.

Coat, waistcoat, and breeches she then did put on,
And a-hunting she went with her dog and her gun;
She hunted around where the farmer did dwell,
Because in her heart she did love him full well.

She oftentimes fired, but nothing she killed,
At length the young farmer came into the field;
And as to discourse with him was her intent,
With her dog and her gun to meet him she went.

"I thought you had been at the wedding," she cried,
"To wait on the squire, and give him his bride."
"No, sir," said the farmer, "if the truth I may tell,
I'll not give her away, for I love her too well."

"Suppose that the lady should grant you her love?
You know that the squire your rival would prove."
"Why, then," says the farmer, "with sword-blade in hand,
By honour I'll gain her when she shall command."

It pleased the lady to find him so bold;
She gave him a glove that was flowered with gold,
And she told him she found it when coming along,
As she was a-hunting with dog and with gun.

The lady went home with a heart full of love,
And she gave out a notice that she'd lost a glove;
And said, "Who has found it, and brings it to me,
Whoever he is, he my husband shall be."

The farmer was pleased when he heard of the news,
With heart full of joy to the lady he goes.
"Dear honoured lady, I've picked up your glove,
And hope you'll be pleased to grant me your love."

"It already is granted, and I'll be your bride;
I love the sweet breath of a farmer," she cried,
"I'll be mistress of dairy, and milking the cow,
While my jolly brisk farmer sings sweet at the plough."

And when she was married she told of her fun,
And how she went a-hunting with dog and with gun.
"And now I have got him so fast in my snare,
I'll enjoy him forever, I vow and declare."

PRODUCTION NOTES

Technique

Live pantomime in silhouette against a large white screen
drawn across a stage or a wide, open doorway, with a projector light behind the performers.

Cast

Wealthy young squire—Wears rich breeches and coat, with
lace at neck and cuffs.

Nobleman's daughter—Coat, waistcoat, and breeches under
her cloak. Cloak is removed when she is hunting.

Mother—Long dress.

Farmer—Long trousers tucked into high boots, short tunic,
and cardboard sword at waist.

Town crier—Coat and breeches.

Several friends and relatives—Women in long dresses; men in handsome breeches and coats.

Three narrators—Offstage. One for descriptive passages, and one for each speaking part.

Setting

No scenery is necessary. The glove can be a real glove. The dog and gun are made of stiff cardboard. The dog is pulled by a string by the nobleman's daughter.

Action

Projector light goes on. The young squire and the nobleman's daughter are silhouetted against the screen, surrounded by friends and relatives. The farmer comes forward to give the young lady away, but instead they gaze at each other. The nobleman's daughter places her hand over her heart and turns away from the squire. She exits with her mother. Relatives and friends shake their heads. The projector light goes off.

When light goes on again, the lady is dressed as a hunter and carries a rifle. Her dog is at her side. She walks a distance and fires her gun. The farmer appears and she walks toward him with her dog. They speak to each other. The lady gives the farmer her glove. Both exit and the light goes off.

The light is turned on. A town crier pretends to read a notice. He is surrounded by a group of people, including the nobleman's daughter. The farmer enters, hears the news, takes the glove from his pocket, and shows it to the young lady. He kneels at her feet. She raises him to his feet and takes both his hands in hers. They then walk off the stage, as the group of people look after them and wave. Projector light goes off.

Moy Castle

ANONYMOUS

There are seven men in Moy Castle
    Are merry men this night;
There are seven men in Moy Castle
    Whose hearts are gay and light.

Prince Charlie came to Moy Castle
    And asked for shelter there,
And down came Lady M'Intosh,
    As proud as she was fair.

"I'm a hunted man, Lady M'Intosh—
    A price is on my head!
If Lord Loudon knew thou'dst sheltered me,
    Both thou and I were sped."

"Come in! come in, my prince!" said she,
    And opened wide the gate;
"To die with Prince Charlie Stuart,
    I ask no better fate."

She's called her seven trusty men,
    The blacksmith at their head:
"Ye shall keep watch in the castle wood,
    To save our prince from dread."

The lady has led the prince away,
  To make him royal cheer;
The seven men of M'Intosh
  Have sought the forest drear.

And there they looked and listened,
  Listened and looked amain;
And they heard the sound of the falling leaves,
  And the soft sound of the rain.

The blacksmith knelt beside an oak,
  And laid his ear to the ground,
And under the noises of the wood
  He heard a distant sound.

He heard the sound of many feet,
  Warily treading the heather—
He heard the sound of many men
  Marching softly together.

"There's no time now to warn the prince,
  The castle guards are few;
'Tis wit will win the play tonight,
  And what we here can do."

He's gi'en the word to his six brethren,
  And through the wood they're gone;
The seven men of M'Intosh
  Each stood by himself alone.

"And he who has the pipes at his back,
   His best now let him play;
And he who has no pipes at his back,
   His best word let him say."

It was five hundred Englishmen
   Were treading the purple heather,
Five hundred of Lord Loudon's men
   Marching softly together.

"There's none tonight in Moy Castle
   But servants poor and old;
If we bring the prince to Loudon's lord,
   He'll fill our hands with gold."

They came lightly on their way,
   Had never a thought of ill,
When suddenly from the darksome wood
   Broke out a whistle shrill.

And straight the wood was filled with cries,
   With shouts of angry men,
And the angry skirl of the bagpipes
   Came answering the shouts again.

The Englishmen looked and listened,
   Listened and looked amain.
And nought could they see through the mirk night,
   But the pipes shrieked out again.

"Hark to the slogan of Lochiel,
    To Keppoch's gathering cry!
Hark to the rising swell that tells
    Clanranald's men are nigh!

"Now woe to the men that told us
    Lochiel was far away!
The whole of the Highland army
    Is waiting to bar our way.

"It's little we'll see of Charlie Stuart,
    And little of Loudon's gold,
And but we're away from this armed wood,
    Our lives have but little hold."

It was five hundred Englishmen,
    They turned their faces and ran,
And well for him with the swiftest foot,
    For he was the lucky man.

And woe to him that was lame or slow,
    For they trampled him on the heather!
And back to the place from whence they came
    They're hirpling all together.

Lord Loudon's men, they are gone full far,
    Over the brow of the hill;
The seven men of M'Intosh,
    Their pipes are crying still.

They leaned them to a tree and laughed,
  'Twould do good to hear,
And they are away to Moy Castle
  To tell their lady dear.

And who but Lady M'Intosh
  Would praise her men so bold?
And who but Prince Charlie Stuart
  Would count the good French gold?

There are seven men in Moy Castle
  Are joyful men this night;
There are seven men in Moy Castle
  Whose hearts will aye be light.

PRODUCTION NOTES

Technique

Puppet stage. Papier-mâché hand puppets. Rod puppets constructed of stiff cardboard represent five hundred Englishmen.

Cast

Seven men—Wear rugged tunics and tights.

Lady M'Intosh—Long flowing gown, pointed cardboard hat with long, filmy veil attached at top.

Prince Charlie—Scotch-plaid kilt with a plaid sash across his shoulder, and a tam o'shanter.

Four narrators—Offstage. One reads descriptive passages,

while others read speaking parts. All narrators participate when noise and shouting are indicated.

Setting

The forest scene is made of painted cardboard trees, shrubs, and rocks attached to the stage floor. Goblets are made of construction paper. Sound effects are a bagpipe playing, marching feet, and a shrill whistle. A recording of bagpipes can be played.

Action

Before drawn curtains, the seven men of Moy Castle appear from below stage, holding goblets. They drink and dance to the sound of bagpipes. Prince Charlie enters from the left; the music stops and the men stop dancing. Lady M'Intosh enters from the right and encourages the prince to come in. Then she turns to the leader and instructs him. The prince and the lady exit at the right and the seven men at the left.

The curtains open. The seven men wait in the forest. One of them, a blacksmith, kneels beside a tree. There is the faint sound of marching feet, which gets louder. The blacksmith gestures to the other men, and they hide behind trees and rocks. Many rod-puppet soldiers approach. There is a shrill whistle, which signals the playing of bagpipes. Then there are angry cries from the lady's men, and the stage is filled with confusion and noise. The marching Englishmen, who believe the whole Highland army is close, are frightened. They turn around and exit. After they leave, the seven men of Moy Castle come out. They are laughing, and the pipes are still playing. The curtains are drawn.

128

The seven men reappear before closed curtains, back at Moy Castle. While the bagpipes are still playing softly, Prince Charlie and Lady M'Intosh reappear. The lady praises her men by nodding her head and waving to them as they dance and make merry.

A Note on the Stories

This section is devoted to stories: fables, folk tales, modern stories, and Bible stories.

Fables are stories that tell about moral behaviour, which are sometimes written in verse but mostly in prose. They make use of animals who talk and act as people do. There are two main sources of fables: the Greek fables of Aesop, and the *Panchatantra* (*Five Books*), a collection from India. Aesop's fables are attributed to a Greek slave of the sixth century B.C. The animals in Aesop's fables speak and act as people do, but they never lose their basic animal characteristics. For example, in *The Hare and the Tortoise* the hare is fast and the tortoise slow. Each uses his own natural qualities to develop the fable.

In the Hindu fables of the *Panchatantra* the animals do not behave like animals but rather like human beings. They could almost be human beings wearing animal masks. For example, in *The Tiger, The Brâhman, and The Jackal* the jackal uses his wit in much the same way that a clever human being would. Because of their simple dramatic quality, many of these fables are perfect for puppetry.

Folk tales are old stories that have existed for hundreds of years. They were told by people all over the world and handed down from generation to generation by word of mouth.

Some scholars believe folk tales began with our Indo-European ancestors and travelled with people as they migrated. Other scholars believe the same tales originated among different peoples in different places of the world at the same time. They base their belief on the theory that people are the same the world over and have basically the same ideas, experiences, and reactions.

Whatever the origin of the folk tales, people told these stories wherever they met—whether it was in the market-places or around the hearths in their homes—not only to entertain but to explain human behaviour. Folk tales give us insight. But they do more than that. They administer justice. In them, the young, the weak, and the poor overcome the odds against them. Through them, also, we are given the power to conquer evil and the opportunity to strive for goodness. There are folk tales about magic and enchantment, wit and perseverance, talking animals, tasks and trials, honest fools who are rewarded, wishes, trickery, and races. This drama of life is challenged by the artistry of the puppet stage!

Most folk tales have a simple style. Because of the simplicity and dramatic qualities of these tales, they lend themselves very well to puppetry. Here are ready-made stories that can be narrated and acted out with puppets of all kinds.

Modern stories are every bit as exciting, humorous, romantic, and imaginative as folk and fairy tales. These stories are more believable than fables and folk tales, for everything that happens could happen.

Sometimes sections of long fictional stories lend themselves to puppetry, but this is not usual, since there is so much description and detail involved in developing the story. One must be careful to choose selections in which something is always happening, as in Charles Dickens's *A Christmas Carol*. Almost any section in this classic is suitable for the puppet stage. There are also such stories as *The Story of Ferdinand* and *Georgie's Halloween*, both dramatic and short, which can be narrated in their entirety for the puppet stage.

The Bible is a very rich source of material for puppet shows. It contains many different forms of writing, including hero tales, biography, songs, proverbs, poetry, philosophy, romance, and history. Its vocabulary is rich, it is written with direct, rhythmical language, and it is filled with beautiful imagery. Selections from the Bible should be simple stories having dramatic narrative continuity rather than philosophical ideas.

The Hare and the Tortoise

AESOP

The Hare was once boasting of his speed before the other animals. "I have never yet been beaten," said he, "when I put forth my full speed. I challenge anyone here to race with me."

The Tortoise said quietly, "I accept your challenge."

"That is a good joke," said the Hare. "I could dance round you all the way."

131

"Keep your boasting till you've beaten," answered the Tortoise. "Shall we race?"

So a course was fixed and a start was made. The Hare darted almost out of sight at once, but soon stopped and, to show his contempt for the Tortoise, lay down to have a nap.

The Tortoise plodded on and plodded on; and when the Hare awoke from his nap, he saw the Tortoise nearing the winning post but the Hare could not run up in time to save the race.

PRODUCTION NOTES

Technique

Puppet stage. Sock puppets. The hare is a long, heavy white sock with long construction-paper ears attached to it. The nose and mouth are pieces of pink felt pasted to the toe. Whiskers are pieces of whisk-broom straw pasted under the nose. The tortoise is a long, heavy grey sock. Pieces of felt pasted to the toe are eyes, nose, and mouth. The rest of the sock is decorated with pieces of small diamond-shaped coloured felt pasted over it. For complete directions on making such puppets, see page 36.

Papier-mâché hand puppets may be used instead.

Use rod puppets for the woodland animals.

Cast

Hare

Tortoise

One narrator—Offstage. Reads entire story. However, several people backstage should cheer when the tortoise wins.

Setting

There are trees and bushes and a road constructed of stiff cardboard and painted. A countryside scene is painted on the backdrop.

Action

The curtain opens. The hare and the tortoise, surrounded by woodland animals, speak to each other at one end of the stage. When the race begins, the woodland animals disappear below stage. The hare and the tortoise begin to run, the tortoise moving slowly. The hare lies down to sleep, and shortly afterwards the tortoise reaches the finish line at the opposite side of the stage. The woodland animals appear at the finish line from below the stage as the tortoise wins, and they cheer. Curtain is closed.

The Fox and the Grapes

AESOP

One hot summer's day a Fox was strolling through an orchard. He came to a bunch of grapes just ripening on a vine that had been trained over a lofty branch.

"Just the thing to quench my thirst," quoth the Fox.

Drawing back a few paces, he took a run and a jump, but just missed the bunch. Turning round again with a one, two, three! he jumped up, but with no greater success.

Again and again he tried after the tempting morsel, but at last had to give it up. He walked away with his nose in the air, saying, "I am sure the grapes are sour."

133

PRODUCTION NOTES

Technique

Puppet stage. Rod-puppet shadow play behind a white screen, with a projector light behind the puppets. Shown in profile, puppets are cut out of flat cardboard.

Cast

Fox

One narrator—Offstage.

Setting

A grape arbour, in silhouette, with several bunches of grapes hanging from it, is attached to the floor of the stage behind the screen. It is made of stiff cardboard.

Action

Projector light goes on. The fox enters slowly, stops before the grapevine and looks up. He then backs up a few paces, runs, and jumps up, trying to snatch a bunch of grapes. He does this several times, then gives up and slowly walks away. Projector light goes off.

The Lion and the Mouse

AESOP

Once when a Lion was asleep a little Mouse began running up and down upon him; this soon wakened the Lion, who placed his huge paw upon him, and opened his big jaws to swallow him.

134

"Pardon, O King," cried the little Mouse. "Forgive me this time, and I shall never forget it. Who knows but what I may be able to do you a turn some of these days?"

The Lion was so tickled at the idea of the Mouse being able to help him, that he lifted up his paw and let the Mouse go.

Some time after this the Lion was caught in a trap, and the hunters, who desired to carry him alive to the King, tied him to a tree while they went in search of a wagon to carry him in.

Just then the little Mouse happened to pass by, and seeing the sad plight in which the Lion was, went up to him and soon gnawed away the ropes that bound the King of the Beasts.

"Was I not right?" said the little Mouse. "Little friends may prove great friends."

PRODUCTION NOTES

Technique

Puppet stage. Papier-mâché hand puppets.

Cast

Lion—Tan cloth with bushy mane and tail made of yarn.

Mouse—Grey costume with little pink felt ears attached to head.

Two hunters—Green outfits with green caps.

Two narrators—Offstage. One for descriptive passages, and another for the mouse.

135

Setting

A forest scene in the background. A tree and several bushes, made of cardboard and painted, are in the foreground.

Action

The curtain opens. A lion is stretched out, fast asleep. A mouse is running up and down on him. The lion stops the mouse, they make their agreement, and the mouse exits. Two hunters appear. One carries a rope with a noose at the end. They creep up on the lion quietly and trap him by throwing

The lion

the noose around his neck and pulling. They tie the lion to
the tree, and leave. The mouse enters and, pretending to
gnaw away the rope, he lifts the noose off the lion's head
and frees him. The lion and the mouse shake paws. Curtain
closes.

Androcles and the Lion

TRANSLATED FROM APION,
THE AEGYPTIACA

Androcles, a runaway slave, had fled to a forest for safety.
He had not been there long when he saw a Lion who was
groaning with pain. He started to flee, but when he realized
that the Lion did not follow but only kept on groaning,
Androcles turned and went to it. The Lion, instead of rush-
ing at him, put out a torn and bloody paw. Androcles, seeing
the poor beast was in pain and wanting to help it, went up,
took its paw, and examined it. Discovering a large thorn, the
man pulled it out and thus relieved the pain. The grateful
Lion in return took Androcles to its cave and every day
brought him food. Sometime later both were captured and
taken to Rome. The slave was condemned to be killed by
being thrown to the Lion, which had not had food for several days. Androcles was led into the arena in the presence
of the Emperor and his court, and at the same time the Lion
was loosed. It came headlong toward its prey, but when it
came near Androcles, instead of pouncing upon him, it
jumped up and fawned upon him like a friendly dog. The

Emperor was much surprised and called to him Androcles who told his story. The Emperor freed both the slave and the Lion, for he thought such kindness and such gratitude were deserving of reward.

PRODUCTION NOTES

Technique
Puppet stage. Papier-mâché hand puppets.

Cast
Androcles—Wears a short white Roman toga.
Emperor—White toga with purple robe over it.
Emperor's courtiers—Loose white togas.
Lion—Costume is made of tan cloth. Bushy mane is made by pasting yarn on his head. Tail made of yarn.
One narrator—Offstage.

Setting
Two sets are used: the cave and the circus. The cave has bushes around it. The circus arena, on stage left, has a platform on which the emperor sits. The cave, bushes, circus arena, and platform are made of stiff cardboard, painted, and pasted to the floor of the stage.

Action
Curtain opens. The lion is lying in front of the cave, groaning pitifully. Androcles pulls the thorn out of his paw, pulling hard as the narrator repeats the word "pulled." The lion rubs his head against Androcles to show gratitude before leading the man to his cave. The captors enter the forest

138

stealthily. Each carries a rope with a noose at one end. They capture the lion and Androcles and lead them to the arena. The emperor and his courtiers appear for the circus. Androcles and the lion are led separately into the arena. The lion recognizes Androcles, goes up to him and rubs his head against him to show affection. The emperor frees them both. Androcles shakes the lion's paw. Curtain closes.

The Tiger, the Brâhman, and the Jackal

FLORA ANNIE STEEL

Once upon a time a tiger was caught in a trap. He tried in vain to get out through the bars, and rolled and bit with rage and grief when he failed.

By chance a poor Brâhman came by. "Let me out of this cage, O pious one!" cried the tiger.

"Nay, my friend," replied the Brâhman mildly, "you would probably eat me if I did."

"Not at all!" swore the tiger with many oaths; "on the contrary, I should be forever grateful, and serve you as a slave!"

Now when the tiger sobbed and sighed and wept and swore, the pious Brâhman's heart softened, and at last he consented to open the door of the cage. "What a fool you are! What is to prevent my eating you now, for after being cooped up so long I am just terribly hungry!"

In vain the Brâhman pleaded for his life; the most he could

139

gain was a promise to abide by the decision of the first three things he chose to question as to the justice of the tiger's action.

So the Brâhman first asked a pipal tree what it thought of the matter, but the pipal tree replied coldly, "What have you to complain about? Don't I give shade and shelter to every one who passes by, and don't they in return tear down my branches to feed their cattle? Don't whimper—be a man!"

Then the Brâhman, sad at heart, went farther afield till he saw a buffalo turning a well-wheel; but he fared no better for it, for it answered, "You are a fool to expect gratitude! Look at me! While I gave milk, they fed me on cotton-seed and oil-cake; but now I am dry they yoke me here, and give me refuse as fodder!"

The Brâhman, still more sad, asked the road to give him its opinion.

"My dear sir," said the road, "how foolish you are to expect anything else! Here am I, useful to everybody, yet all, rich and poor, great and small, trample on me as they go past, giving me nothing but the ashes of their pipes and the husks of their grain!"

On this the Brâhman turned back sorrowfully, and on the way he met a jackal, who called out, "Why, what's the matter, Mr. Brâhman? You look as miserable as a fish out of water!"

Then the Brâhman told him all that had occurred. "How very confusing!" said the jackal, when the recital was ended. "Would you mind telling me over again? For everything seems so mixed up!"

The Brâhman told it all over again, but the jackal shook

140

his head in a distracted sort of way, and still could not under-stand.

"It's very odd," said he sadly, "but it all seems to go in at one ear and out at the other! I will go to the place where it all happened, and then perhaps I shall be able to give a judgment."

So they returned to the cage, by which the tiger was wait-ing for the Brâhman, and sharpening his teeth and claws.

"You've been away a long time!" growled the savage beast, "but now let us begin our dinner."

"Our dinner!" thought the wretched Brâhman, as his knees knocked together with fright. "What a remarkably delicate way of putting it!"

"Give me five minutes, my lord," he pleaded, "in order that I may explain matters to the jackal here, who is some-what slow in his wits."

The tiger consented, and the Brâhman began the whole story over again, not missing a single detail, and spinning as long a yarn as possible.

"Oh, my poor brain! oh, my poor brain!" cried the jackal, wringing his paws. "Let me see! how did it all begin? You were in the cage, and the tiger came walking by——"

"Pooh!" interrupted the tiger, "what a fool you are! *I* was in the cage."

"Of course!" cried the jackal, pretending to tremble with fright; "yes! I was in the cage—no, I wasn't—dear! dear! Where are my wits? Let me see—the tiger was in the Brâh-man, and the cage came walking by—no, that's not it either! Well, don't mind me, but begin your dinner, for I shall never understand!"

"Yes, you shall!" returned the tiger, in a rage at the jackal's stupidity; "I'll make you understand! Look here—I am the tiger——"

"Yes, my lord!"

"And that is the Brâhman——"

"And that is the cage——"

"Yes, my lord!"

"And I was in the cage—do you understand?"

"Yes—no—please my lord——"

"Well?" cried the tiger, impatiently.

"Please, my lord!—How did you get in?"

"How?—why, in the usual way, of course!"

"Oh dear me!—my head is beginning to whirl again! Please don't be angry, my lord, but what is the usual way?"

At this the tiger lost patience, and, jumping into the cage, cried, "This way! Now do you understand how it was?"

"Perfectly!" grinned the jackal, as he dexterously shut the door, "and if you will permit me to say so, I think matters will remain as they were!"

PRODUCTION NOTES

Technique

Live pantomime in front of a large white screen or sheet. Each character wears a mask. Masks are made of cartridge paper, decorated, and tied on to cover the face.

Cast

Brâhman—Wears white, loosely draped sheet and mask.
Tiger—Dark tights with tail, shirt, mask, and mittens.

Some masks performers can wear

Buffalo—Dark tights with tail, shirt, mask, and mittens.
Jackal—Dark tights with tail, shirt, mask, and mittens.
Seven narrators—Offstage. One for descriptive passages, and one for each speaking part, including the road and the pipal tree.

Setting

On the far right there is a water well, and in the middle, a road and a tree. A scene of a forest can be attached to the white screen in the background. Props for the cage, the tree, the road, and the water well, with a turning wheel attached, are constructed of stiff cardboard and painted. The full-sized cage has a door attached with slackened masking tape, which can be opened and closed. The cage is on the left side of the stage.

Action

Performers take their places in front of the screen while the floodlights are still out. When the lights are turned on, the tiger is walking back and forth angrily in the cage, roaring with rage. Then he pauses to shake the bars. He cannot escape, which makes him angrier. The Brâhman is a simple, timid man. He stops, speaks to the tiger, then opens the cage. The tiger leaps out and threatens to eat the Brâhman, who is frightened. His shoulders droop, and he shakes his head and walks slowly away after the tiger fools him. He stops to speak to the tree, the buffalo, and the road. Then he meets the jackal.

The jackal pretends his poor brain does not function, pointing to his head and wringing his paws. He is also humble before the mighty tiger. When the tiger is fooled and re-enters his cage, the jackal quickly shuts the door and, for the first time, shows how clever he is. He puts his paw on the Brâhman's shoulder as they walk off the stage. When the floodlights are turned off, the tiger roars louder.

The Three Bears

ROBERT SOUTHEY

Once upon a time there were Three Bears, who lived together in a house of their own in a wood. One of them was a Little, Small, Wee Bear; and one was a Middle-sized Bear; and the other was a Great, Huge Bear. They had each a pot for their porridge: a little pot for the Little, Small, Wee Bear; and a middle-sized pot for the Middle Bear; and a great pot for the Great, Huge Bear. And they had each a chair to sit in: a little chair for the Little, Small, Wee Bear; and a middle-sized chair for the Middle Bear; and a great chair for the Great, Huge Bear. And they had each a bed to sleep in: a little bed for the Little, Small, Wee Bear; and a middle-sized bed for the Middle Bear; and a great bed for the Great, Huge Bear.

One day after they had made the porridge for their breakfast and poured it into their porridge-pots they walked out into the wood while the porridge was cooling, that they might not burn their mouths by beginning too soon to eat it. And while they were walking a little old Woman came to the house. First she looked in at the window, and then she peeped in at the keyhole; and, seeing nobody in the house, she lifted the latch. The door was not fastened, because the Bears were good Bears, who did nobody any harm and never suspected

* Some authorities believe "The Three Bears" was published between 1834 and 1837. Others say it was written by an anonymous author in 1831 and retold by Southey. This is the story on which *Goldilocks and the Three Bears* is based.

that anybody would harm them. So the little old Woman opened the door and went in, and well pleased she was when she saw the porridge on the table. If she had been a good little old Woman she would have waited till the Bears came home, and then, perhaps, they would have asked her to breakfast, for they were good Bears—a little rough or so, as the manner of Bears is, but for all that very good-natured and hospitable. But she was an impudent old Woman, and set about helping herself.

So first she tasted the porridge of the Great, Huge Bear, and that was too hot for her. And then she tasted the porridge of the Middle Bear, and that was too cold for her. And then she went to the porridge of the Little, Small, Wee Bear, and tasted that; and that was neither too hot nor too cold, but just right; and she liked it so well that she ate it all up.

Then the little old Woman sat down in the chair of the Great, Huge Bear, and that was too hard for her. And then she sat down in the chair of the Middle Bear, and that was too soft for her. And then she sat down in the chair of the Little, Small, Wee Bear, and that was neither too hard nor too soft, but just right. So she seated herself in it, and there she sat till the bottom of the chair came out, and down she came, plump upon the ground.

Then the little old Woman went upstairs into the bed-chamber in which the Three Bears slept. And first she lay down upon the bed of the Great, Huge Bear, but that was too high at the head for her. And next she lay down upon the bed of the Middle Bear, and that was too high at the foot for her. And then she lay down upon the bed of the Little, Small, Wee Bear, and that was neither too high at the head nor at the foot, but just right. So she covered herself up comfortably and lay there till she fell fast asleep.

By this time the Three Bears thought their porridge would be cool enough, so they came home to breakfast. Now, the little old Woman had left the spoon of the Great, Huge Bear standing in his porridge.

"SOMEBODY HAS BEEN AT MY PORRIDGE!" said the Great, Huge Bear, in his great, rough, gruff voice. And when the Middle Bear looked at his he saw that the spoon was standing in it too.

"Somebody has been at my porridge!" said the Middle Bear, in his middle voice.

Then the Little, Small, Wee Bear looked at his, and there was the spoon in the porridge-pot, but the porridge was all gone.

"Somebody has been at my porridge, and has eaten it all up!" said the Little, Small, Wee Bear, in his little, small, wee voice.

Upon this the Three Bears, seeing that some one had entered their house and eaten up the Little, Small, Wee Bear's breakfast, began to look about them. Now, the little old Woman had not put the hard cushion straight when she rose from the chair of the Great, Huge Bear.

"SOMEBODY HAS BEEN SITTING IN MY CHAIR!" said the Great, Huge Bear, in his great, rough, gruff voice.

And the little old Woman had squatted down the soft cushion of the Middle Bear.

"Somebody has been sitting in my chair!" said the Middle Bear, in his middle voice.

And you know what the little old Woman had done to the third chair.

"Somebody has been sitting in my chair, and has sat the

147

bottom out of it!" said the Little, Small, Wee Bear, in his little, small, wee voice.

Then the Three Bears thought it necessary that they should make further search; so they went upstairs into their bedchamber. Now, the little old Woman had pulled the pillow of the Great, Huge Bear out of its place.

"SOMEBODY HAS BEEN LYING IN MY BED!" said the Great, Huge Bear, in his great, rough, gruff voice.

And the little old Woman had pulled the bolster of the Middle Bear out of its place.

"Somebody has been lying in my bed!" said the Middle Bear, in his middle voice.

And when the Little, Small, Wee Bear came to look at his bed there was the little old Woman.

"Somebody has been lying in my bed—and here she is!" said the Little, Small, Wee Bear, in his little, small, wee voice.

The little old Woman had heard in her sleep the great, rough, gruff voice of the Great, Huge Bear; but she was so fast asleep that it was no more to her than the roaring of wind or the rumbling of thunder. And she had heard the middle voice of the Middle Bear, but it was only as if she had heard some one speaking in a dream. But when she heard the little, small, wee voice of the Little, Small, Wee Bear it was so sharp and so shrill that it awakened her at once. Up she started; and when she saw the Three Bears on one side of the bed she tumbled herself out of the other and ran to the window. Now, the window was open, because the Bears always opened their bedchamber window when they got up in the morning. Out the little old Woman jumped and the Three Bears never saw anything more of her.

PRODUCTION NOTES

Technique

Puppet stage. Papier-mâché hand puppets.

Cast

Old woman—Wears apron and cap.

Big bear—Dark-brown bear suit.

Middle-sized bear—Same as big bear.

Small bear—Same as big bear.

Five narrators—Offstage. One reads descriptive passages, and others read the speaking parts.

Setting

Interior of the bears' house. On the far right there is a closed door. On the far left, three beds: a small one, a middle-sized one, and a big one, each with a cover and pillow. In the centre there is a cloth-covered table with three bowls and spoons on it. Three chairs are around the table: small, medium and large, each covered with a cushion. The background has a cut-out window with curtains attached.

The table, chairs, and beds are made of stiff cardboard. The closed door, also made of cardboard, is attached to the side of the stage with slackened broad masking tape so it can open. A small screw serves as a knob and a keyhole is painted on the door.

Action

Curtain opens. The little old woman appears from below the puppet stage and peers through the window. Only her head can be seen as she looks out at the audience. She then comes around to the front of the puppet stage and peeks through the keyhole of the door. She pulls the door open

149

and walks in. She tries each bear's porridge and finally eats the entire contents of the small bowl. She sits in the chairs, disarranging the cushions of the first two and breaking the bottom of the third. She goes to the left-hand corner of the puppet stage and tries the beds. She falls asleep in the small bed. The bears return. They look at their porridge bowls, then examine the chairs, and finally go to the bedroom, walking from bed to bed until they find the old woman. She is awakened and jumps out of the window by going to the window and simply disappearing below stage. Curtain closes.

Johnny-Cake

JOSEPH JACOBS

Once upon a time there was an old man, and an old woman, and a little boy. One morning the old woman made a Johnny-cake, and put it in the oven to bake. "You watch the Johnny-cake while your father and I go out to work in the garden." So the old man and the old woman went out and began to hoe potatoes, and left the little boy to tend the oven. But he didn't watch it all the time, and all of a sudden he heard a noise, and he looked up and the oven door popped open, and out of the oven jumped Johnny-cake, and went rolling along end over end, towards the open door of the house. The little boy ran to shut the door, but Johnny-cake was too quick for him and rolled through the door, down the steps, and out into the road long before the little boy could catch him. The little boy ran after him as fast as he could clip it, crying out to his father and mother, who heard the uproar and threw down their hoes and gave chase too. But Johnny-cake outran all three a long way, and was soon out of sight, while they had to sit down, all out of breath, on a bank to rest.

On went Johnny-cake, and by-and-by he came to two well-diggers who looked up from their work and called out: "Where ye going, Johnny-cake?"

He said: "I've outrun an old man, and an old woman, and a little boy, and I can outrun you too-o-o!"

"Ye can, can ye? we'll see about that!" said they; and they threw down their picks and ran after him, but couldn't catch up with him, and soon they had to sit down by the roadside to rest.

On ran Johnny-cake, and by-and-by he came to two ditch-diggers who were digging a ditch. "Where ye going, Johnny-cake?" said they. He said: "I've outrun an old man, and an old woman, and a little boy, and two well-diggers, and I can outrun you too-o-o!"

"Ye can, can ye? we'll see about that!" said they; and they threw down their spades, and ran after him too. But Johnny-cake soon outstripped them also, and seeing they could never catch him, they gave up the chase and sat down to rest.

On went Johnny-cake, and by-and-by he came to a bear. The bear said: "Where ye going, Johnny-cake?"

He said: "I've outrun an old man, and an old woman, and a little boy, and two well-diggers, and two ditch-diggers, and I can outrun you too-o-o!"

"Ye can, can ye?" growled the bear, "we'll see about that!" and trotted as fast as his legs could carry him after Johnny-cake, who never stopped to look behind him. Before long the bear was left so far behind that he saw he might as well give up the hunt first as last, so he stretched himself out by the roadside to rest.

On went Johnny-cake, and by-and-by he came to a wolf. The wolf said: "Where ye going, Johnny-cake?"

He said: "I've outrun an old man, and an old woman, and a little boy, and two well-diggers, and two ditch-diggers, and a bear, and I can outrun you too-o-o!"

"Ye can, can ye?" snarled the wolf, "we'll see about that!" And he set into a gallop after Johnny-cake, who went on and on so fast that the wolf too saw there was no hope of over-taking him, and he too lay down to rest.

On went Johnny-cake, and by-and-by he came to a fox that lay quietly in a corner of the fence. The fox called out in a sharp voice, but without getting up: "Where ye going, Johnny-cake?"

He said: "I've outrun an old man, and an old woman, and a little boy, and two well-diggers, and two ditch-diggers, a bear, and a wolf, and I can outrun you too-o-o!"

The fox said: "I can't quite hear you, Johnny-cake, won't you come a little closer?" turning his head a little to one side.

Johnny-cake stopped his race for the first time, and went a little closer, and called out in a very loud voice: "I've out-run an old man, and an old woman, and a little boy, and two well-diggers, and two ditch-diggers, and a bear, and a wolf, and I can outrun you too-o-o."

"Can't quite hear you; won't you come a little closer?" said the fox in a feeble voice, as he stretched out his neck towards Johnny-cake, and put one paw behind his ear.

Johnny-cake came up close, and leaning towards the fox screamed out: "I'VE OUTRUN AN OLD MAN, AND AN OLD WOMAN, AND A LITTLE BOY, AND TWO WELL-DIGGERS, AND TWO DITCH-DIGGERS, AND A BEAR, AND A WOLF, AND I CAN OUTRUN YOU TOO-O-O!"

"You can, can you?" yelped the fox, and he snapped up the Johnny-cake in his sharp teeth in the twinkling of an eye.

PRODUCTION NOTES

Technique

Puppet stage. Papier-mâché hand puppets or stuffed paper-bag puppets for human characters. Johnny-cake is made of a long, heavy tan sock, with polyurethane at the heel end for his head. Pierce a hole in the polyurethane for your index finger and tie a ribbon under the head to keep polyurethane in place. Fold the toe of the sock over the polyurethane for a cap. Paste pieces of coloured felt on for eyes, nose, and mouth. The bear, wolf, and fox are small paper-bag puppets. The bottoms of the bags fold over and open and close like mouths. Decorate appropriately with pieces of coloured felt.

Cast

Old man—Wears shirt and hat.

Old woman—Apron and kerchief.

153

The fox

Little boy—No hat.
Two well diggers—Dressed like old man.
Two ditch diggers—Dressed like old man.
Bear
Wolf
Fox
Johnny-cake
Ten narrators—Offstage. One for descriptive passages, and one for each speaking part.

154

Setting

The interior of a cottage is located on the far left. An oven is painted on the left-hand background scene. There is an open door with a flight of stairs leading from it. On the far right, there is a white fence. An outdoor scene is painted on the right-hand backdrop. A garden patch is in the middle. For the scene that takes place indoors, the floodlight shines on the far left. For the outdoor scene, the floodlight switches to the right, leaving the cottage interior in dim light. All overhead lights are out. Stairs are constructed of cardboard. Small hoes, picks, spades, and a fence are made of stiff cardboard.

Action

The old woman walks to the oven in the background and pretends to put Johnny-cake into the oven, and then she speaks to the boy. She and her husband go out to the garden. When the oven door is supposed to pop open, the Johnny-cake puppet appears from below stage. Johnny-cake runs to the door. The little boy tries to shut the door, but Johnny-cake quickly runs down the stairs, and past the garden, with the boy, the woman, and the man chasing him.

He runs to the right side of the stage. The boy, woman, and man sit down to rest. They all disappear below stage. Johnny-cake runs back and forth several times, each time meeting another group and outrunning them. They all give up, sitting down and then disappearing below stage. Finally the fox catches Johnny-cake and holds him in his mouth. Johnny-cake quickly disappears below stage. Curtain closes.

The Three Billy-Goats-Gruff

PETER CHRISTEN ASBJORNSEN

TRANSLATED BY G. W. DASENT

Once on a time there were three Billy-Goats who were to go up to the hillside to make themselves fat, and the family name of the three goats was "Gruff."

On the way up was a bridge, over a burn they had to cross; and under the bridge lived a great ugly Troll, with eyes as big as saucers and a nose as long as a poker.

First of all came the youngest Billy-Goat-Gruff to cross the bridge.

"Trip, trap! Trip, trap!" went the bridge.

"WHO'S THAT tripping over my bridge?" roared the Troll.

"Oh! it is only I, the tiniest Billy-Goat-Gruff; and I'm going up to the hillside to make myself fat," said the Billy-Goat, with such a small voice.

"Now, I'm coming to gobble you up," said the Troll.

"Oh, no! pray don't take me. I'm too little, that I am," said the Billy-Goat. "Wait a bit till the second Billy-Goat-Gruff comes; he's much bigger."

"Well! be off with you," said the Troll.

A little while after came the second Billy-Goat-Gruff to cross the bridge.

"Trip, trap! Trip, trap!" went the bridge.

"WHO'S THAT tripping over my bridge?" roared the Troll.

"Oh! it's the second Billy-Goat-Gruff, and I'm going up to

the hillside to make myself fat," said the Billy-Goat, who hadn't such a small voice.

"Now, I'm coming to gobble you up," said the Troll.

"Oh, no! don't take me. Wait a little till the big Billy-Goat-Gruff comes; he's much bigger."

"Very well; be off with you," said the Troll.

But just then up came the big Billy-Goat-Gruff.

"*Trip, Trap! Trip, Trap!*" went the bridge, for the Billy-Goat was so heavy that the bridge creaked and groaned under him.

"WHO'S THAT tramping over my bridge?" roared the Troll.

"It's I! THE BIG BILLY-GOAT-GRUFF," said the Billy-Goat, who had a big hoarse voice of his own.

"Now, I'm coming to gobble you up," roared the Troll.

> "Well, come along! I've got two spears,
> And I'll poke your eyeballs out at your ears,
> I've got besides two curling-stones,
> And I'll crush you to bits, body and bones."

That was what the big Billy-Goat said; so he flew at the Troll and poked his eyes out with his horns, and crushed him to bits, body and bones, and tossed him out into the burn, and after that he went up to the hillside. There the Billy-Goats got so fat they were scarcely able to walk home again; and if the fat hasn't fallen off them, why they're still fat; and so—

> Snip, snap, snout,
> This tale's told out.

PRODUCTION NOTES

Technique

Puppet stage. Rod-puppet shadow play behind a screen, with a projector light behind the puppets. Shown in profile, puppets are cut out of cardboard. Troll has a very long nose and one large cut-out circle for his eye. The projector light shining through the eye opening will make the Troll seem alive and frightening. Each Billy-Goat-Gruff is larger than the one preceding him, and each has horns extending from his forehead. Papier-mâché hand puppets may also be used.

Cast

Small Billy-Goat-Gruff
Medium Billy-Goat-Gruff
Big Billy-Goat-Gruff
Troll
Five narrators—Offstage. One reads the descriptive passages, while the others read the speaking parts.

Setting

Silhouetted against the screen is a bridge spanning a brook. On the left side of the bridge is a lowland; on the right side is a high, grassy hill. The curved bridge is made of stiff cardboard. Water under the bridge is stiff scalloped cardboard to create the effect of a rippling brook. The water-edge plants at both ends of the bridge and the grass on the hill are also made of cardboard. Props are attached to a table, which serves as the floor of the stage.

Action

Projector light goes on. The first two Billy-Goats-Gruff are

158

frightened. They move slowly and cautiously as they walk over the bridge. When the Troll shouts, the puppeteer shakes the goats to make them tremble. The big Billy-Goat-Gruff is not afraid. He shouts back at the Troll. When the Troll appears from under the bridge, the big Billy-Goat-Gruff fights him and finally tosses him into the brook. The victor then crosses the bridge to the grassy hill, and all three Billy-Goats-Gruff eat contentedly. Projector light goes off.

The Shepherd's Pipe

RETOLD BY ROSE LAURA MINCIELI

It was a cold winter night. The stars were shining brightly in the sky and the earth was sleeping under a soft, white blanket of snow. It had just been announced that a little Bambino had been born in a stable. Many people came from far and near to visit the Child, and they brought with them simple gifts to lay before Him. Some brought bread and cheese freshly made that very morning, some brought ricotta, olives, and figs, and there were those who brought baby lambs and new-born rabbits.

Among the travellers was a poor young shepherd who felt very sad because he had nothing which he could give to the Bambino. All he had in the world was a shepherd's pipe which he had made to while away the lonely hours while tending the sheep in the fields. After travelling for a

159

long, long time and feeling very tired, he finally arrived at the stable where the Bambino was lying in a manger. He knelt in the farthest corner of the stable, hoping he would not be seen, and held in his hands his shepherd's pipe. But the Child's mother saw him. She went to the corner where he knelt, took him by the hand, and led him to the manger where her Son lay wrapped in swaddling clothes.

The good shepherd, feeling welcomed by the mother's kindness, took heart and said to her, "But I have no gift to give to the Bambino save perhaps a little tune from my shepherd's pipe."

"That would be splendid," said the mother, smiling kindly. But just as the shepherd was about to play on his pipe, who should enter but Three Kings dressed in their royal splendour, bearing rich gifts of gold, myrrh, and frank- incense. When the poor shepherd saw such splendid gifts, he withdrew from the manger to make way for the three men of wealth and returned to his corner where he was con- tent to stay. But the good mother looked at him and said softly, "Come closer to the manger for the Bambino cannot hear your music if you play it so far away."

The shepherd, encouraged once more, passed before the Three Kings of royal splendour and stood before the Bam- bino's manger. He played upon his shepherd's pipe the sweetest lullaby ever heard. And there came within the stable a silence while all listened to the little tune. The Kings were silent, the shepherds and peasants were silent—even the lambs and rabbits and birds and cows and chickens and donkeys were silent while the shepherd played.

The music from the pipe was as sweet and melodious as

the crooning voice of all the mothers in the world singing to their babies.

The little Babe heard the music and turned His eyes to look upon the shepherd who played to Him. The Bambino looked long and kindly at the shepherd and there came upon him a great feeling of peace and good will. He made music such as never had been heard before. When he stopped playing, the mother went to him, placed her hand upon his curly, black hair, and smiled at him.

When the shepherd walked out of the stable and passed the rich Kings and merchants, they all bowed before him, for he had given the most precious gift to the Bambino—music played from his heart.

PRODUCTION NOTES

Technique
Puppet stage. Papier-mâché hand puppets. Accompanied by the music of "Silent Night" on a recorder or record.

Cast
Two villagers—Wear coarse robes.
Shepherd—Coarse robes.
Bambino—Small doll in swaddling clothes with outstretched arms.
Bambino's Mother—Loosely draped white garment; veil over head and shoulders.
Three Kings—Velvet robes and gold crowns, made of cardboard and covered with gold foil. One carries a small box of

jewels; another, a small box of myrrh; and the third, a small goblet of frankincense. The boxes are covered with aluminium foil.

One narrator—Offstage. Reads entire story.

Setting

Interior of a stable on the left with wooden rafters overhead. Clustered around the manger are a cow, a donkey, and chickens. Stars attached to strings hang from the top of the proscenium. The animals are made of cardboard and attached to the floor of the stage. Birds are made of cardboard and attached to wooden rafters. The manger is made of wood and contains straw. The shepherd's pipe is a small piece of bamboo, notched on one side. A small searchlight is focused on the travellers and then on the interior of the stable.

Action

Curtains open. Bambino's mother kneels, gazing at Him. Villagers enter slowly from right and place their gifts before the manger. Then the shepherd enters from right and retreats to a corner. He comes forward but retreats again when he sees the Three Kings, who also enter from right. The Three Kings walk slowly and with much dignity into the stable, and place their gifts before the manger. Later the shepherd is urged to stand beside the manger, and plays on his pipe. The narrator, or another person, could play a Christmas song while the shepherd plays. Curtain closes.

162

Peter and the Wolf

SERGEI PROKOFIEV

Early one morning Peter opened the gate and went out into the big green meadow. On the branch of a birch tree sat a little bird—Peter's friend. When he saw Peter he chirped at him gaily, "All's quiet here."

Soon a duck came waddling around. She was very happy to see that Peter had not closed the gate, and so decided to have a nice swim in the deep pond in the meadow. As soon as the little bird saw the duck, he flew down and settled himself in the grass beside her. Shrugging his shoulders he said, "What kind of a bird are *you* if you can't fly?" To which the duck replied, "What kind of a bird are *you* if you can't swim?" and dived into the pond. They argued and argued, the duck swimming in the pond, the little bird hopping back and forth along the bank. Suddenly, something caught Peter's eye.

It was a cat crawling through the grass. The cat said to herself, "The bird is busy arguing. If I could only have him for my dinner!" Stealthily she crept toward him on her velvet paws.

"Oh, look out!" cried Peter.

Quickly the bird flew up into the tree while the duck quacked angrily at the cat—from the middle of the pond. The cat crawled round and round the tree and thought, "Is it worth climbing up so high? By the time I get there the bird will have flown away."

163

All at once Grandpapa came out. He was angry because Peter had gone to the meadow. "The meadow is a dangerous place," he cried. "What if a wolf should come out of the forest?—What would you do then?" Peter paid no attention to Grandpapa's words.

Boys like Peter are not afraid of wolves. Grandpapa took Peter by the hand, led him home—and locked the gate.

No sooner had Peter gone than a big grey wolf *did* come out of the forest. In a twinkling the cat sprang up into the tree. The duck quacked and in her great excitement jumped out of the pond.

No matter how hard the duck tried to run, she couldn't escape the wolf. He was getting nearer and nearer. He was catching up with her—there—he got her—and swallowed her with a single gulp!

And now this is how things stood: the cat was sitting on one branch up in the tree, the bird was sitting on another—not too close to the cat, while the wolf walked round and round the tree, looking at them both with greedy eyes. In the meantime, Peter, without the slightest fear, stood behind the closed gate, watching all that was going on. Presently, he ran into the house, found a strong rope, hurried back and climbed up the high stone wall. One of the branches of the tree, around which the wolf was pacing stretched out over this high wall. Grabbing hold of this branch, Peter climbed over into the tree. He said to the bird, "Fly down and circle around the wolf's head, but take care that he doesn't catch you!" The bird almost touched the wolf's head with his wings, while the wolf snapped furiously at him from this side—and that. How that bird did worry the wolf! And oh! how the wolf tried to catch him! But the bird was far too clever for him.

Meanwhile, Peter had made a lasso, and letting it down very carefully—he caught the wolf by the tail and pulled with all his might. Feeling himself caught, the wolf began to jump wildly, trying to get loose. But Peter had tied the other end of the rope to the tree, and the wolf's jumping only made the rope tighter around his tail! Just then, who should come out of the woods but the hunters who were following the wolf's trail, and shooting as they came. From his perch in the tree Peter cried out to them: "You don't need to shoot. The bird and I have already caught him! Please help us take him to the zoo."

The hunters were only too willing. And now you can just imagine the triumphant procession! Peter at the head—after him the hunters, leading the wolf—and winding up the procession, Grandpapa and the cat. Grandpapa shook his head reprovingly. "This is all very well, but what if Peter had *not* caught the wolf—what then!" Above them flew the little bird, merrily chirping, "Aren't we smart, Peter and I? See what *we* have caught!" And if you had listened very carefully, you could have heard the duck quacking away inside the wolf, because in his haste the wolf had swallowed her whole—and the duck was still alive.

PRODUCTION NOTES

Technique

Puppet stage. Several different kinds of hand puppet may be used. Peter and Grandfather are papier-mâché hand puppets. The hunters, the cat, the duck, and the bird are rod puppets, cut out in action poses. The wolf is an empty paper bag, with its mouth at the bottom of the bag.

Also effective is live pantomime, either in front of a screen, with performers wearing masks, or in silhouette behind a screen, with a projector light behind the performers.

A performance may be accompanied by the musical interpretation of "Peter and the Wolf," by Sergei Prokofiev. In the record, a narrator tells the story, and a different musical instrument is used to represent each of the characters.

Cast
Peter—Wears a short jacket and a cap.
Grandfather—Dressed like Peter.
Two or three hunters—Dressed like Peter. Carry guns.
Bird
Duck
Cat
Wolf
Six narrators—Offstage. One reads descriptive passages, while the others read the dialogue.

Setting
A meadow. A birch tree is on the left. A stone wall is close to the tree; a pond is in the centre; and a gate is on the right. Grass and flowers are painted on the backdrop. Two pots of fern, one each side of the stage, complete the setting. The pond is made of crumpled aluminium foil. The birch tree and gate are constructed of stiff cardboard and painted. The gate, attached with slackened masking tape, opens and closes. Peter's lasso is a cord with a noose at one end.

Action

Curtains open. The bird sits on the branch of the birch tree, while a cat lurks nearby. Peter enters from below stage and opens the gate. The bird speaks to Peter. Then the duck appears, and the animals argue, while the cat stealthily creeps toward the bird.

Peter quickly warns the bird, which flies up into the tree. Grandfather enters, takes Peter by the hand, and takes him away, scolding all the time. Both disappear below stage.

The wolf enters and chases the duck, which waddles from side to side as it attempts to escape. After the wolf captures and swallows the duck (which disappears below stage), he circles the tree, considering the possibility of capturing the cat, which has jumped up into the tree, and the bird, too.

Peter enters and runs back beyond the gate and below stage. He returns with a lasso and approaches the tree on which the bird is perched. He whispers his plan to capture the wolf.

The bird circles the wolf's head, but does not get close enough to be caught. Peter catches the wolf by the tail with his lasso and pulls the animal up, by putting the rope over the branch of the tree.

Shots are heard and the hunters appear. They are about to shoot the wolf, but Peter persuades them to reconsider. Then a procession forms, as they prepare to deliver the wolf to the zoo. Peter is at the head. Behind him are the hunters with the captured wolf, then Grandfather and the cat. The bird follows overhead. Curtain closes.

167

Christmas With the Cratchits

CHARLES DICKENS

Then up rose Mrs. Cratchit, Cratchit's wife, dressed out but poorly in a twice-turned gown but brave in ribbons, which are cheap and make a goodly show for sixpence; and she laid the cloth, assisted by Belinda Cratchit, second of her daughters, also brave in ribbons; while Master Peter Cratchit plunged a fork into the saucepan of potatoes, and getting the corners of his monstrous shirt collar (Bob's private property, conferred upon his son and heir in honour of the day) into his mouth, rejoiced to find himself so gallantly attired and yearned to show his linen in the fashionable parks.

And now two smaller Cratchits, boy and girl, came tearing in, screaming that outside the baker's they had smelled the goose, and known it for their own. And basking in luxurious thoughts of sage and onion, these young Cratchits danced about the table and exalted Master Peter Cratchit to the skies, while he (not proud, although his collar nearly choked him) blew the fire until the slow potatoes, bubbling up, knocked loudly at the saucepan lid to be let out and peeled.

"What has ever got your precious father then?" said Mrs. Cratchit. "And your brother, Tiny Tim! And Martha warn't as late last Christmas Day by half an hour!"

"Here's Martha, Mother!" said a girl, appearing as she spoke.

"Here's Martha, Mother!" cried the two young Cratchits. "Hurrah! There's *such* a goose, Martha!"

"Why, bless your heart alive, my dear, how late you are!" said Mrs. Cratchit, kissing her a dozen times and taking off her shawl and bonnet for her with officious zeal.

"We'd a deal of work to finish up last night," replied the girl, "and had to clear away this morning, Mother!"

"Well! Never mind so long as you are come," said Mrs. Cratchit. "Sit ye down before the fire, my dear, and have a warm, Lord bless ye!"

"No, no! There's Father coming," cried the two young Cratchits, who were everywhere at once. "Hide, Martha, hide!"

So Martha hid herself, and in came little Bob, the father, with at least three feet of comforter exclusive of the fringe, darned up and brushed to look seasonable; and Tiny Tim upon his shoulder. Alas for Tiny Tim, he bore a little crutch, and had his limbs supported by an iron frame!

"Why, where's our Martha?" cried Bob Cratchit, looking round.

"Not coming," said Mrs. Cratchit.

"Not coming!" said Bob, with a sudden declension in his high spirits; for he had been Tim's blood horse all the way from church and had come home rampant. "Not coming upon Christmas Day!"

Martha didn't like to see him disappointed, if it were only in joke; so she came out prematurely from behind the closet door and ran into his arms, while the two young Cratchits hustled Tiny Tim and bore him off into the wash house that he might hear the pudding singing in the copper.

"And how did little Tim behave?" asked Mrs. Cratchit, when she had rallied Bob on his credulity and Bob had hugged his daughter to his heart's content.

"As good as gold," said Bob, "and better. Somehow he gets thoughtful, sitting by himself so much, and thinks the strangest things you ever heard. He told me, coming home, that he hoped the people saw him in the church, because he was a cripple and it might be pleasant to them to remember upon Christmas Day who made lame beggars walk and blind men see."

Bob's voice was tremulous when he told them this, and trembled more when he said that Tiny Tim was growing strong and hearty.

His active little crutch was heard upon the floor, and back came Tiny Tim before another word was spoken; escorted by his brother and sister to his stool before the fire; and while Bob, turning his cuffs—as if, poor fellow, they were capable of being made more shabby—compounded some hot mixture in a jug and stirred it round and round and put it on the hob to simmer, Master Peter and the two ubiquitous young Cratchits went to fetch the goose, with which they soon returned in high procession.

Such a bustle ensued that you might have thought a goose the rarest of all birds, a feathered phenomenon, to which a black swan was a matter of course—and in truth it was something very like it in that house. Mrs. Cratchit made the gravy (ready beforehand in a little saucepan) hissing hot; Master Peter mashed the potatoes with incredible vigour;

Miss Belinda sweetened up the apple sauce; Martha dusted the hot plates; Bob took Tiny Tim beside him in a tiny corner to the table; the two young Cratchits set chairs for everybody, not forgetting themselves, and mounting guard upon their posts, crammed spoons into their mouths lest they should shriek for goose before their turn came to be helped.

At last the dishes were set on and grace was said. It was succeeded by a breathless pause as Mrs. Cratchit, looking slowly all along the carving knife, prepared to plunge it in the breast; but when she did and when the long expected gush of stuffing issued forth, one murmur of delight arose all around the board, and even Tiny Tim, excited by the two young Cratchits, beat on the table with the handle of his knife and feebly cried, "Hurrah!"

There never was such a goose. Bob said he didn't believe there ever was such a goose cooked. Its tenderness and flavour, size and cheapness, were the themes of universal admiration. Eked out by the apple sauce and mashed potatoes, it was a sufficient dinner for the whole family; indeed, as Mrs. Cratchit said with great delight (surveying one small atom of a bone upon the dish) they hadn't eaten it all at last! Yet everyone had had enough, and the youngest Cratchits in particular were steeped in sage and onion to the eyebrows! But now, the plates being changed by Miss Belinda, Mrs. Cratchit left the room alone—too nervous to bear witness—to take the pudding up and bring it in.

Suppose it should not be done enough! Suppose it should break in turning out! Suppose somebody should have got over the wall of the back yard and stolen it while they were merry with the goose—a supposition at which the two young Cratchits became livid! All sorts of horrors were supposed.

Hallo! A great deal of steam! The pudding was out of the copper. A smell like a washing day! That was the cloth. A smell like an eating house and a pastry cook's next door to each other, with a laundress's next door to that! That was the pudding! In half a minute Mrs. Cratchit entered—flushed but smiling proudly—with the pudding, like a speckled cannon ball, so hard and firm, blazing in half of half-a-quartern of ignited brandy, and bedight with Christmas holly stuck into the top.

Oh, a wonderful pudding! Bob Cratchit said, and calmly too, that he regarded it as the greatest success achieved by Mrs. Cratchit since their marriage. Mrs. Cratchit said that now the weight was off her mind she would confess she had had her doubts about the quantity of flour. Everybody had something to say about it, but nobody said or thought it was at all a small pudding for a large family. It would have been flat heresy to do so. Any Cratchit would have blushed to hint at such a thing.

At last the dinner was all done, the cloth was cleared, the hearth swept, and the fire made up. The compound in the jug being tasted and considered perfect, apples and oranges were put upon the table and a shovelful of chestnuts on the fire. Then all the Cratchit family drew around the hearth in what Bob Cratchit called a circle, meaning half a one; and at Bob Cratchit's elbow stood the family display of glass—two tumblers and a custard cup without a handle.

These held the hot stuff from the jug, however, as well as golden goblets would have done; and Bob served it out with beaming looks, while the chestnuts on the fire sputtered and cracked noisily.

Then Bob proposed, "A Merry Christmas to us all, my dears. God bless us!"

Which all the family re-echoed.

"God bless us every one!" said Tiny Tim, the last of all.

PRODUCTION NOTES

Technique

Live pantomime in silhouette behind a large white screen drawn across a stage or a wide, open doorway, with a projector light behind the performers. Use a small boy for Tiny Tim and a bigger boy for Bob Cratchit.

Cast

Mrs. Cratchit—Wears a shirt with blouse, apron, mob cap and ribbons.

Bob Cratchit—Tight trousers, shirt with a high wing collar, long jacket. When he enters, he is also wearing a long woollen scarf around his neck and a high hat, which is made of stiff cardboard.

Tiny Tim—Shabby but neat trousers, Eaton cap made of stiff cardboard, wooden crutch. Also wears a scarf when he enters.

Belinda Cratchit—Dressed like Mrs. Cratchit.

Martha Cratchit—Dressed like Mrs. Cratchit.

Smaller Cratchit girl—Also dressed like Mrs. Cratchit.

Peter Cratchit—Dressed like Bob Cratchit.

173

Smaller Cratchit boy—Breeches, stockings, and long jacket. Seven narrators—Offstage. One for descriptive passages, and one for each speaking part.

Setting
Interior of Cratchit's home. The silhouette of a dinner table appears in the centre, and there are seven chairs. On the table there are Christmas candles and a tablecloth.

The cardboard fireplace, in the right-hand corner, has a hook from which a jug hangs. Nearby is a stool. On a small

Bob Cratchit

stand near the fireplace, there are two tumblers and a cup without a handle.

The goose, brought in later, is made of papier-mâché. The Christmas pudding, also papier-mâché, has a piece of holly on top. Other props are several place settings, glasses, apples, oranges, and chestnuts. Wax fruit may be used.

One side of the screen serves as the street entrance; the other leads to and from the kitchen.

Action

Projector light goes on. Mrs. Cratchit and Belinda set the dinner table, bringing in the necessary items from the kitchen. The narrator pauses briefly to give them time to complete the task. Martha dusts the plates with a dishcloth. When she learns that her father is coming, she hides in the kitchen.

Bob Cratchit enters from the street side with Tiny Tim on his shoulders. He stops, speaks to his wife, and asks for Martha, who shortly reappears.

The young Cratchits leave to fetch the goose, then return, carrying it on a platter and walking as though they were taking part in an important ceremony. They place the goose on the table with a flourish, and everyone takes a chair and sits at the table.

As the narrator reads Bob Cratchit's dialogue during the Christmas dinner, the eldest boy shakes his head and waves his hands to express his delight. Mrs. Cratchit leaves and then returns with the plum pudding.

Later, the young Cratchits go into the kitchen and return with apples, oranges, and chestnuts. They place the fruit on the table and the chestnuts in the fireplace. All the Cratchits draw their chairs around the fireplace and sit down. Tiny Tim sits on his stool.

Bob Cratchit takes the two tumblers and custard cup from the small table beside the fireplace, passes the cups around, and proposes a Christmas toast. The projector lights go off as the cups are upraised.

Noah's Ark

THE BIBLE: GENESIS 6, 7, 8 (Abridged)

And God said unto Noah, "The end of all flesh is come before me; for the earth is filled with violence through them; and, behold, I will destroy them with the earth.

"Make thee an ark of gopher wood; rooms shalt thou make in the ark, and shalt pitch it within and without with pitch.

"And this is the fashion which thou shalt make it of; the length of the ark shall be three hundred cubits, the breadth of it fifty cubits, and the height of it thirty cubits.

"And window shalt thou make to the ark, and in a cubit shalt thou finish it above. And the door of the ark shalt thou set in the side thereof; with lower, second, and third stories shalt thou make it.

"And, behold, I, even I, do bring a flood of waters upon the earth, to destroy all flesh, wherein is the breath of life, from under heaven; and everything that is in the earth shall die.

"But with thee will I establish my covenant. And thou

176

shalt come into the ark, thou, and thy sons, and thy wife, and thy sons' wives with thee.

"And of every living thing of all flesh, two of every sort shalt thou bring into the ark, to keep them alive with thee; they shall be male and female.

"And take thou unto thee of all food that is eaten, and thou shalt gather it to thee; and it shall be for food for thee, and for them."

Thus did Noah; according to all that God commanded him, so did he.

And the Lord said unto Noah, "Come thou and all thy house into the ark; for thee have I seen righteous before me in this generation.

"Of every clean beast thou shalt take to thee by sevens, the male and his female; and of beasts that are not clean by two, the male and his female.

"Of fowls also of the air by sevens, the male and the female; to keep seed alive upon the face of all the earth.

"For yet seven days, and I will cause it to rain upon the earth forty days and forty nights; and every living substance that I have made will I destroy from off the face of the earth."

And Noah did according unto all that the Lord commanded him.

In the selfsame day entered Noah, and Shem, and Ham, and Japheth, the sons of Noah, and Noah's wife, and the three wives of his sons with them, into the ark.

They, and every beast after his kind, and all the cattle after their kind, and every creeping thing that creepeth upon the earth after his kind, every bird of every sort.

And they went in unto Noah into the ark, two and two of

all flesh, wherein is the breath of life.

And they that went in, went in male and female of all flesh, as God had commanded him. And the Lord shut him in.

And the flood was forty days upon the earth.

And every living substance was destroyed which was upon the face of the ground, both man and cattle, and the creeping things, and the fowl of the heaven; and they were destroyed from the earth. And Noah only remained alive, and they that were with him in the ark.

And God remembered Noah, and every living thing, and all the cattle that was with him in the ark. And God made a wind to pass over the earth, and the waters assuaged.

And the waters decreased continually.

And it came to pass at the end of forty days, that Noah opened the window of the ark which he had made.

He sent forth a dove from him, to see if the waters were abated from off the face of the ground.

But the dove found no rest for the sole of her foot, and she returned unto him into the ark, for the waters were on the face of the whole earth. Then he put forth his hand, and took her, and pulled her in unto him into the ark.

And he stayed yet other seven days; and sent forth the dove; which returned not again unto him any more.

Noah removed the covering of the ark, and looked, and, behold, the face of the ground was dry.

And God spake unto Noah saying, "Go forth of the ark, thou, and thy wife, and thy sons, and thy sons' wives with thee.

"Bring forth with thee every living thing that is with thee, of all flesh, both of fowl, and of cattle, and of every creeping thing that creepeth upon the earth; that they may breed abundantly in the earth, and be fruitful, and multiply upon the earth."

And Noah went forth, and his sons, and his wife, and his sons' wives with him.

Every beast, every creeping thing, and every fowl, and whatsoever creepeth upon the earth, after their kinds, went forth out of the ark.

PRODUCTION NOTES

Technique

Puppet stage. Rod-puppet shadow play behind a white screen, with a projector light behind the puppets. Shown in profile, puppets should be cut out of flat cardboard. Characteristic poses for the animals; Noah, and his family are exaggerated. Noah's hand is outstretched.

Cast

Noah—Wears loose, flowing robe.

Noah's wife—Loose, flowing gown.

Noah's three sons—Dressed like Noah.

Sons' wives—Dressed like Noah's wife.

Two of each kind of animal—doves, fowl, cows, lions, lambs, goats, giraffes, elephants, donkeys, horses, dogs, cats, and so on.

Two narrators—Offstage. One for descriptive passages, the other for the voice of God.

Setting

The story is shown in two parts. No scenery is needed for the first part. In the second part, there is a silhouette of a three-decked ark. Seen from the side, the ark is cut out of stiff cardboard and attached to a holding rod. It has a cut-out window and a door attached with masking tape and tied with a string so that it will open and close. At the appropriate time, a puppeteer below stage pulls the string to close the door.

The ark is held a short distance from the edge of the stage to permit rod puppets to disappear below stage and reappear again when they enter and then leave the ark.

A prop for the water is made of cardboard cut in scallops and attached to a holding rod. The puppeteer moves it higher to show the swelling flood. Christmas-tree tinsel attached to a crossbar on a rod above the stage can be used for rain. During the storm, the puppeteer shakes the streamers. The sound of wind can be made vocally, and the sound of thunder can be made by rattling a thin piece of tin.

Action

Projector light goes on. Noah stands alone, listening to the voice of God. Projector light goes off. When the light is turned on again, Noah, his family, and the animals appear from the sides of the stage, enter the ark through the open doorway, and disappear below stage. Narrator pauses and appropriate music may be played during the procession to permit as many animals as desired to enter the ark.

As they enter the ark, the characters disappear below stage. Later, Noah stands at the cut-out window and sends out the dove, which appears from below stage. The dove flies off and then returns. Noah sends the dove out a second time, but this time it does not return. To show the waters receding, the wave prop is lowered until it disappears.

All characters leave the ark, two by two. The record is played again and the projector light goes off.

David and Goliath

THE BIBLE: 1 SAMUEL, 17 (ABRIDGED)

Now the Philistines gathered together their armies to battle. And Saul and the men of Israel were gathered together, and pitched by the valley of Elah, and set the battle in array against the Philistines.

And the Philistines stood on a mountain on the one side, and Israel stood on a mountain on the other side; and there was a valley between them.

And there went out a champion out of the camp of the Philistines named Goliath, of Gath, whose height was six cubits and a span.

And he had an helmet of brass upon his head, and he was armed with a coat of mail; and the weight of the coat was five thousand shekels of brass.

And he had greaves of brass upon his legs, and a target of brass between his shoulders.

And the staff of his spear was like a weaver's beam; and his spear's head weighed six hundred shekels of iron; and one bearing a shield went before him.

And he stood and cried unto the armies of Israel and said unto them, "Why are ye come out to set your battle in array? Am not I a Philistine, and ye servants to Saul? Choose you a man for you, and let him come down to me.

"If he be able to fight with me, and to kill me, then will we be your servants; but if I prevail against him, and kill him, then shall ye be our servants, and serve us."

And the Philistine said, "I defy the armies of Israel this

day; give me a man, that we may fight together."

When Saul and all Israel heard those words of the Philistine, they were dismayed, and greatly afraid.

Now the three eldest sons of Jesse went and followed Saul to the battle.

And Jesse said unto David his son, "Take now for thy brethren an ephah of this parched corn, and these ten loaves, and run to the camp to thy brethren.

"And carry these ten cheeses unto the captain of their thousand, and look how thy brethren fare, and take their pledge."

And David rose up early in the morning, and left the sheep with a keeper, and took, and went, as Jesse had commanded him; and he came to the trench, as the host was going forth to the fight, and shouted for the battle.

For Israel and the Philistines had put the battle in array, army against army.

And David left his bundle in the hand of the keeper of the baggage, and ran into the army, and came and saluted his brethren.

And as he talked with them, behold, there came up the champion, the Philistine of Gath, Goliath by name, out of the armies of the Philistines, and spake according to the same words; and David heard them.

And all the men of Israel, when they saw the man, fled from him, and were sore afraid.

And the men of Israel said, "Have ye seen this man that is come up? Surely to defy Israel is he come up; and it shall be, that the man who killeth him, the king will enrich him with great riches, and will give him his daughter, and make his father's house free in Israel."

And David spake to the men that stood by him, saying, "What shall be done to the man that killeth this Philistine, and taketh away the reproach from Israel? For who is this Philistine that he should defy the armies of the living God?"

And the people answered him after this manner, saying, "So shall it be done to the man that killeth him."

And Eliab, his eldest brother, heard when he spake unto the men; and Eliab's anger was kindled against David, and he said, "Why camest thou down hither? And with whom has thou left those few sheep in the wilderness? I know thy pride, and the naughtiness of thine heart; for thou are come down that thou mightest see the battle."

And David said, "What have I now done? Is there not a cause?"

And he turned from him toward another, and spake after the same manner; and the people answered him again after the former manner.

And when the words were heard which David spake, they rehearsed them before Saul; and he sent for him.

And David said to Saul, "Let no man's heart fail because of him; thy servant will go and fight with this Philistine."

And Saul said to David, "Thou art not able to go against this Philistine to fight with him; for thou art but a youth, and he a man of war from his youth."

And David said unto Saul, "Thy servant kept his father's sheep, and there came a lion, and a bear, and took a lamb out of the flock.

"And I went out after him, and smote him, and delivered it out of his mouth; and when he arose against me, I caught him by his beard, and smote him, and slew him.

"Thy servant slew both the lion and the bear; and this

Philistine shall be as one of them, seeing that he hath defied the armies of the living God."

David said moreover, "The Lord that delivered me out of the paw of the lion, and out of the paw of the bear, he will deliver out of the hand of this Philistine."

And Saul said unto David, "Go, and the Lord be with thee."

And Saul armed David with his armour, and put an helmet of brass upon his head; also he armed him with a coat of mail.

And David girded his sword upon his armour, and he assayed to go; for he had not proved it.

And David said unto Saul, "I cannot go with these; for I have not proved them." And David put them off him.

And he took his staff in his hand, and chose him five smooth stones out of the brook, and put them in a shepherd's bag which he had, even in a scrip; and his sling was in his hand; and he drew near to the Philistine.

And the Philistine came on and drew near unto David; and the man that bore the shield went before him.

And when the Philistine looked about, and saw David, he disdained him; for he was but a youth, and ruddy, and of fair countenance.

And the Philistine said unto David, "Am I a dog that thou comest to me with staves?" And the Philistine cursed David by his gods.

And the Philistine said to David, "Come to me, and I will give thy flesh unto the fowls of the air, and to the beasts of the field."

Then said David to the Philistine, "Thou comest to me with a sword, and with a spear, and with a shield; but I come to thee in the name of the Lord of hosts, the God of the armies of Israel, whom thou hast defied.

"This day will the Lord deliver thee into mine hand; and I will smite thee, and take thine head from thee, and I will give the carcasses of the host of the Philistines this day unto the fowls of the air, and to the wild beasts of the earth; that all the earth may know that there is a God in Israel.

"And all this assembly shall know that the Lord saveth not with sword and spear; for the battle is the Lord's and he will give you into our hands."

And it came to pass, when the Philistine arose, and came and drew nigh to meet David, that David hasted, and ran toward the army to meet the Philistine.

And David put his hand in his bag, and took thence a stone, and slang it, and smote the Philistine in his forehead, that the stone sunk into his forehead and he fell upon his face to the earth.

So David prevailed over the Philistine with a sling and with a stone, and smote the Philistine, and slew him; but there was no sword in the hand of David.

And when the Philistines saw that their champion was dead, they fled.

And the men of Israel and of Judah arose, and shouted, and pursued the Philistines.

And the children of Israel returned from chasing after the Philistines, and they spoiled their tents.

And when Saul saw David go forth against the Philistine, he said unto Abner, the captain of the host, "Abner, whose son is this youth?" And Abner said, "As thy soul liveth, O king, I cannot tell."

185

And the king said, "Enquire thou whose son the stripling is."

And as David returned from the slaughter of the Philistine, Abner took him, and brought him before Saul.

And Saul said to him, "Whose son art thou young man?"

And David answered, "I am the son of thy servant Jesse the Bethlehemite."

PRODUCTION NOTES

Technique

Puppet stage. Papier-mâché hand puppets. Goliath is very large. David, a boy, is the smallest puppet. For the effect of many soldiers, several cardboard rod puppets are used.

Cast

Goliath—Wears a helmet, coat of mail. All are made of cartridge paper and cardboard covered with aluminium foil. Carries a spear. This may be a pencil covered with aluminium foil. Later carries a cardboard sword.

King Saul—Long, rich robes; crown of cardboard covered with gold foil.

Jesse—Long shepherd's robes. Carries a staff.

David—Short, loose shepherd's garment. Carries a slingshot.

David's three brothers—Dressed like David.

King Saul's keeper and captain—Rich robes. Carry shields.

Goliath's shield bearer—Dressed like Goliath. Carries Goliath's shield.

Soldiers—Cut out of stiff cardboard. Wear helmets, coats of mail. Carry shields.

Goliath

Six narrators—Offstage. One for descriptive passages, and one for each speaking part.

Setting

Most of the action takes place on the battlefield. There is hilly terrain with pitched tents, each of which has a small, bright flag on top. Those on the left belong to the Israelites. Philistine soldiers are camped on the hills to the right. Tents and soldiers are also painted on the backdrop. In the centre there is a deep valley. For a brief period, the action takes place before closed curtains.

Action

The curtain opens. Saul and his men stand on the left near the Israelite camp. Goliath's shield bearer enters from the right, followed by Goliath, who waves his spear and shouts threats. The soldiers of Israel tremble with fear.

The curtain closes and Jesse and David enter. Jesse gives David a bag containing cheese and bread, which David carries over his arm. Both exit.

The curtain opens. David enters the battlefield from the left, gives the keeper the bag, and salutes his brothers. Goliath once more challenges the Israelites, and several of them run off the stage. David asks about the terms of the challenge. This angers his oldest brother, but the boy obtains the information from another soldier.

Saul, who is nearby, hears about David and sends one of his men to bring the boy to him. Waving his arms David tells Saul how he saved his father's sheep. Saul is impressed and points to Goliath, urging David to fight him. A soldier places a helmet on David's head and a coat of mail over his body to prepare him for battle. David removes them and picks up some stones that are lying nearby.

As the battle begins, Goliath approaches the valley from the right and David from the left. They face each other, and the Philistine waves his sword contemptuously when he realizes that his challenger is a shepherd. David lifts his slingshot, throws a stone, and the giant falls. The Philistine soldiers run from the battlefield, with the Israelites in pursuit. David turns back, approaches Saul, and kneels before him. The curtain closes.

The First Christmas

THE BIBLE: ST. LUKE 2: 8-16

And there were in the same country shepherds abiding in the field, keeping watch over their flock by night.

And lo, the angel of the Lord came upon them, and the glory of the Lord shone round about them; and they were afraid.

And the angel said unto them, "Fear not; for, behold, I bring you good tidings of great joy, which shall be to all people.

"For unto you is born this day in the city of David a Saviour, which is Christ the Lord.

"And this shall be a sign unto you; ye shall find the babe wrapped in swaddling clothes, lying in a manger."

And suddenly there was with the angel a multitude of the heavenly host praising God, and saying, "Glory to God in the highest, and on earth peace, good will toward men."

And it came to pass, as the angels were gone away from them into heaven, the shepherds said one to another, "Let us now go even unto Bethlehem, and see this thing which is come to pass, which the Lord hath made known unto us."

And they came with haste, and found Mary, and Joseph, and the babe lying in a manger.

PRODUCTION NOTES

Technique

Puppet stage. Rod puppets behind a white screen, with a

projector light behind the puppets. Shown in profile, all puppets are cut out of stiff cardboard. One shepherd stands with his arms outstretched; one leans on his staff; another shades his eyes with his hand.

Cast

Several shepherds—Wear long, loose robes.
Several small angels—Have outstretched wings.
One large angel—Has outstretched wings.
Mary—Long, loose gown.
Joseph—Long, loose robe.
Babe—This is a small doll with outstretched arms.
Eight narrators—Offstage. One reads descriptive passages, while the others read dialogue.

Setting

The outline of a sloping roof can be seen in the far right. The area of the stage beneath this roof is the interior of the stable. Above the roof are many small stars and one large star. All props are made of cardboard. Stars are hung from above the stage.

Action

Projector light goes on. On the far right, in the interior of the stable, Mary and Joseph kneel beside the Babe in the manger. A group of shepherds are standing on the left-hand side of the stage, tending their sheep. A large angel appears and speaks to the shepherds. Then several small angels appear briefly, after which all the angels disappear from the stage. The shepherds begin to move in the direction of the stable. A Christmas carol plays while they travel. Projector light goes off.

190

Index of Titles

Androcles and the Lion, 137
Apple-Seed John, 59
Babushka, 78
Bailiff's Daughter of Islington, The, 107
Blind Men and the Elephant, The, 37
Christmas With the Crachits, 168
Crow and the Fox, The, 35
David and Goliath, 181
Dumb Wife Cured, The, 90
First Christmas, The, 189
Fox and the Grapes, The, 133
Get Up and Bar the Door, 86
Golden Glove, The, 119
Hare and the Tortoise, The, 131
Johnny-Cake, 150
Lady Clare, 114
Leak in the Dike, The, 51
Lion and the Mouse, The, 134
Little Bo-peep, 28
Little Drummer Boy, 71
Little Jack Horner, 21
Little Miss Muffet, 22
Lochinvar, 111
Mary's Lamb, 24

Molly Malone, 94
Moy Castle, 123
Noah's Ark, 176
Old King Cole, 23
Old Woman Who Lived in a Shoe, The, 30
Peter and the Wolf, 163
Punch and Judy, 19
Robin Hood and Little John, 100
Shepherd's Pipe, The, 159
Singing Leaves, The, 65
Sir Eglamour, 96
Solomon and the Bees, 48
There was an Old Woman, 26
Three Bears, The, 145
Three Billy-Goats-Gruff, The, 156
Three Kings, The, 73
Three Little Kittens, The, 31
Tiger, the Brâhman, and the Jackal, The, 139
Visit from St. Nicholas, A, 82
Where are You Going, My Pretty Maid, 34
Youth and the North Wind, The, 40